**to
make
my
name
good**

to make my name good

A Reexamination of the Southern Kwakiutl Potlatch

Philip Drucker
and
Robert F. Heizer

UNIVERSITY OF CALIFORNIA PRESS
BERKELEY AND LOS ANGELES 1967

UNIVERSITY OF CALIFORNIA PRESS
BERKELEY AND LOS ANGELES, CALIFORNIA

CAMBRIDGE UNIVERSITY PRESS
LONDON, ENGLAND

COPYRIGHT © 1967, BY
THE REGENTS OF THE UNIVERSITY OF CALIFORNIA
LIBRARY OF CONGRESS CATALOG CARD NUMBER: 67-16839

Contents

Introduction	1
Southern Kwakiutl Society	10
Influences of the Historic Period	13
Changes in Potlatch Procedures	35
The Question of the Double Return of the Potlatch Gift	53
Potlatch Controls and Other Mechanisms	81
The Rivalries	98
The Rivalry Gesture	118
The Verbalization of Conflict in the Potlatch	125
The Mortuary Potlatch	130
Conclusion	133
Bibliography	155
Index	159

Introduction

This study presents some hitherto unpublished material on the potlatch complex of the Southern Kwakiutl Indians of British Columbia, and certain conclusions as to the way that institution functioned are derived from this material.[1] There is a considerable literature on the Kwakiutl potlatch, but nonetheless the complex has not been well understood. In fact it has remained an anomaly even in relation to the potlatch customs of neighboring Northwest Coast groups. Because of its volume, published material precisely from the Southern Kwakiutl is used by those who wish to make long-range interareal comparisons or to draw broad theoretical conclusions—a procedure which cannot fail to introduce error. Even such able scholars as Herskovits (1952:164-165, and passim) and Bohannon (1963:253-259) have fallen into this trap owing to the deficiencies of their source material. For this reason it seems worthwhile to present the information at our disposal, which we believe will clarify the picture.

Chronologically speaking, the first important accounts of Southern Kwakiutl potlatching were those published by Franz Boas in 1897. His first intensive investigations, after brief preliminary contacts, began about 1890. He was at the important center of Fort Rupert at times when potlatches and other festi-

[1] Preparation of the present paper was made possible by a grant from the Committee on Research of the University of California (Berkeley). Field work on which it is based was carried out by Drucker aided by grants from the University of California (Culture Element Distribution Survey, 1936–37), the Smithsonian Institution, the Arctic Institute, and the American Philosophical Society (1953). On his departure from the Smithsonian Institution, Drucker deposited all his field notes and like materials in the Archives of the Bureau of American Ethnology, Smithsonian Institution, so that they might be available to anyone who might be interested in them. Special thanks are due to the late Director of the Bureau of American Ethnology, Dr. Frank H. H. Roberts, Jr., for his courtesy in providing us with copies of pertinent notebooks for use in preparing this report. We also wish to express our thanks to Dr. H. G. Barnett, Dr. E. Hammel, and Dr. E. Colson for their valuable, constructive criticisms of a preliminary draft of this discussion.

vals were in progress, observing them with an interpreter at his side. He collected verbatim accounts of the proceedings in the Kwakiutl tongue, later carefully translating them; and he trained his principal interpreter, George Hunt, to record data in phonetic symbols which were then sent to Boas during the periods when he himself could not be in the field. As a result, over the years Boas was able to publish a tremendous quantity of data on the Southern Kwakiutl—on the material, social, and religious aspects of their culture, as well as on their folklore and language. Perhaps no other native American group is so fully and systematically documented.[2] Yet it is just this material that fails us when we try to understand what the Indians were really doing in the performance of an institution of maximum importance to them, the potlatch. It is quite clear that Boas was not interested in developing an internally consistent, functional picture of a cultural complex.

The foregoing might be taken to indicate that we propose to mount an attack not only on Boas' presentation but on his methodology and his theoretical position on the study of culture as well. This is not our intention. We do not have the conceit to believe that a brief study and a few pages of text could refute Boas' fifty years of carefully planned, intensive study of the Southern Kwakiutl. What we do believe we can do is to present a body of significantly complementary material derived by approach through another line of interest and another methodology.

We hold to the view that there are three fundamental categories of ethnographic truth. Stripped of elaborate verbiage, they can be defined simply as: 1, what people say they do; 2, what they believe they do; and 3, what they actually do. Categories 1 and 2 may have a high degree of coincidence, as may 2 and 3 (1 and 3, or 1, 2, and 3 rarely coincide). With or without coincidences, all three of these ethnographic facts and, moreover, the nature and degree of differences between them are meaningful. Some fairly recent essays on Boas' method and scientific philosophy by Wike (1957), Smith (1959), and Codere

[2] Codere (1950, 1959) gives full bibliographies of Boas' works dealing with the Kwakiutl.

(1959) make plain that his chief interest was in the second category—perhaps the most difficult to get at and the most subtle of the three—and that he was to some degree interested also in the first category. This was the reason for his emphasis on the culture of the Indian as seen by the Indian himself. In his zeal for scientific objectivity, Boas was distrustful of the third category, where at times the ethnographer must interject appraisals. We, however, hold that this is a calculated risk that must be taken. Where they must be made, appraisals should, of course, be made as objectively and as devoid of ethnocentric bias as possible, on the ground that all three categories of ethnographic fact, especially where they diverge, are ultimately meaningful and are necessary yardsticks by which to gauge each other. This is our principal difference in theoretical position from that of Boas—perhaps not so vastly different basically—and our main reason for becoming involved in a discussion of this controversial theme.

Boas' early major publications on the Southern Kwakiutl were in print when an independent work on these people was published by E. S. Curtis in his deluxe series, *The North American Indian* (1915, vol. 10). This study sharply contradicts certain of Boas' generalizations on the workings of the potlatch and offers a rather more intelligible picture of that institution, although still not a complete one. However, the vehicle in which this account appears, a very expensive series in limited edition, invariably hidden away in rare book rooms by libraries, has hindered its availability, so that it has not been cited by students as often as it should have been.

Ruth Benedict (1932, 1934), in her attempt to achieve psychological insight into culture, used the Southern Kwakiutl as one of her test cases, basing her study on Boas' materials. For her analysis she drew heavily on data on the potlatch, especially on one special form, the rivalry situation. We are not going to discuss her theory here, but we do want to emphasize that we believe that such defects as her interpretation of Kwakiutl culture may have can be demonstrated to stem as much from misconstruction of the potlatch complex as from flaws in her basic hypothesis.

In a brief but significant paper, "The Function of the Potlatch," Barnett (1938) injected intelligibility into the workings of the complex in terms of its entire distribution on the Northwest Coast. His conclusions apply as completely to the Southern Kwakiutl as to any other group of the area, as he makes clear; but since he did not belabor the point this aspect of his contribution has been overlooked by some students. The same author gives much more detailed consideration to the Southern Kwakiutl institution in his lengthier treatment of the same subject (Barnett, n.d.) which regrettably he has not published.

In 1950 Helen Codere presented a reappraisal of the Southern Kwakiutl potlatch based mainly on two lots of source material, Boas' data, published and unpublished, and historic records such as the annual reports of Indian agents. These latter she utilized with consummate skill to develop the theme of acculturative changes among the Southern Kwakiutl and resultant changes in the potlatch itself. That she did not succeed in resolving the problem of the actual functional operation of the potlatch may be attributed to her reliance on Boas' data, which she did not have the opportunity to supplement by field work based on her interest in acculturative change. Boas' materials did not lend themselves to her approach, because Boas was not studying culture change and acculturation; he did not try to attain a time perspective since he was occupied with quite different problems. There were numerous significant changes in the Southern Kwakiutl potlatch during the lengthy period of his observations, which must have come to his notice but which he did not record.[3] In later papers based on her own field research, Codere (1956, 1957) presents some significant new material, although she does not use it to modify her original conclusions.

In these pages we shall refer frequently to Codere's summaries of historical data, as well as to certain of her conclusions with which our data are in accord. Our data and interpretations coincide closely with her appraisal of the potlatch as a cultural manifestation, not a psychopathological one. There are, how-

---

[3] See Codere (1959:68).

ever, certain major aspects of the problem in which our materials point to conclusions very different from those she reached. However, the present paper is not intended as a critique of her work, but is the presentation of independently collected data and its analysis. In a later study (1961), Codere presents a well-balanced account of Southern Kwakiutl culture in transition, from early historic contacts with white civilization until modern times. Here, the potlatch is considered as an important focus of interest to the Indians, but the mechanics of its operation are not discussed at length. Many of Codere's conclusions as to effects of the acculturation situation on the potlatch will be drawn on in the following pages.

Suttles (1960a, 1960b) has published on the potlatch complex, extending data from certain Coast Salish groups to derive theoretical conclusions as to functions and origins of the entire complex on the Northwest Coast. His approach is a novel one and will require comment, which, however, will be deferred until the Southern Kwakiutl material has been presented. Vayda (1961) and Piddocke (1965) attempt still broader applications of Suttles' hypothesis.

The field data on which our report is based were collected by Drucker in the course of two visits to the Southern Kwakiutl. The first was in 1937 when he spent brief periods at Quatsino Sound with Koskimo informants and at Fort Rupert, with the Kwagyuł[4] His work on this occasion was in connection with the University of California Culture Element Distribution surveys. On such topics as social organization, ceremonials, the potlatch, and the like, Drucker used the usual ethnographic techniques of inquiry—asking informants for general and sequential descriptions, specific cases, and so forth—rather than the more restrictive element-list type of query, having received

[4] The use of the same name for various entities causes some difficulty in presentation, particularly since the tribal and confederacy name has been extended to the linguistic division. In these pages the simplified spelling, "Kwakiutl," is used for the linguistic division, "Southern Kwakiutl" being a dialectic division of the Kwakiutl language which includes Heiltsuk-Haisla. The confederacy of tribes at Fort Rupert is referred to here as "Kwagyuł." The same rendering, uncapitalized, is used for the tribal designations, the kwagyuł (gwetala), and the walas kwagyuł.

Dr. A. L. Kroeber's permission to deviate from the routine element-list technique in these special areas. As a result, he collected a limited body of new information on the potlatch, but one that bristled with leads for further investigation. In 1953 Drucker once more made contact with the Southern Kwakiutl at Alert Bay in the course of the study of an aspect of acculturation among the Indians of British Columbia. This time he explored the topic of the potlatch at some length; acculturation among the Southern Kwakiutl and the recent history of their potlatching are parts of the same story. Subsequently, in two general discussions of Northwest Coast culture,[5] Drucker drew on these data, still in his notebooks, to make certain sweeping generalizations about the potlatch complex. His source material was available only to himself. He was doing what poker players sometimes refer to as "sandbagging," a lucrative but rather unsporting operation. His participation in the present work will, he trusts, remedy this situation.

Drucker's principal Southern Kwakiutl informants were two: Charles E. Nowell and Ed Whonnuck. Mr. Nowell's partial biography, which does not altogether do him justice, was published by C. S. Ford (1941) under the title *Smoke from Their Fires*. Intellectually and in personality, Nowell was an unusual man. He respected tradition and sought not only to comply with the forms of Kwakiutl custom but to understand their meaning as well, but at the same time he was able to make a better than usual adjustment to the stresses and strains of the bitter phase of acculturation that persisted most of his lifetime. He participated intensively in the potlatch; as a youth he used his superior schooling, for a Kwakiutl of his generation, to act as scribe and potlatch bookkeeper for his elder brother and other chiefs as well. Throughout his working life Nowell consistently earned a better than average (Indian) income by working at jobs of special responsibility and trust in the canneries; he was active in the organization of the first effective Indian union on the coast (the Pacific Coast Native Fishermen's Association). He was influential, although no longer so active be-

[5] Drucker, 1955; 1965.

cause of his age, in the activities of the Native Brotherhood of British Columbia, with which the Southern Kwakiutl became affiliated. He had been Drucker's main informant at Fort Rupert in 1937, so when the two met again in 1953 there was a background of former friendship that created an excellent rapport.

Mr. Whonnuck[6] was in some respects a different sort of person, although he too was a man who had made a good adjustment to the bicultural situation. If some of his forebears had been social climbers in times when the traditional rigidity of Kwakiutl social structure had been weakened by various acculturative forces, they had achieved high status for him; his right to various important titles and positions in the potlatch system was unchallenged. He had been active in the potlatch throughout his adult life. He was also a successful fisherman, owner of a large seine boat that represented a considerable capital investment and normally provided him with a good income. A still energetic man, Whonnuck probably would not have been available as an informant had he not been incapacitated with a leg injury. He was at first rather impatient with the informant's role but, as the interviews continued, came to find it an interesting way to pass the time. Well informed on a wide range of subjects related to modern Kwakiutl culture, from the potlatch to trade unionism in the fishing industry, he expressed his views clearly and sometimes rather picturesquely.

These two men contrasted in an interesting way, which made their contributions of data especially valuable since they consistently corroborated each other's statements (they were interviewed separately, of course). Mr. Nowell was the scholar, the philosopher of his own culture; Mr. Whonnuck was the hardboiled pragmatist. It is worth noting that they were friends, and in fact Mr. Nowell recommended Mr. Whonnuck to the ethnographer as an expert on the subject of the potlatch.

In addition, Drucker collected information in 1937 from Quatsino Sam, and in 1953 from Mr. Dan Cranmer at Alert Bay and Chief Billy Assu of the Lekwiltok.

[6] The surname has various renderings. Drucker understood that this version is that used by the family at present. It derives from a Heiltsuk name, wɔnuq, said to mean "river owner."

A brief summary of the social significance of the potlatch in this area will set the stage for our discussion. The term "potlatch" derives from Chinook jargon and means simply "to give." (All discussants of the potlatch must make this statement; it is the only thing we all agree on!) Each linguistic division, from the Tlingit to the groups of western Washington, had its own term, or actually terms, to refer to various forms of the potlatch and to distinguish these affairs from feasts. A potlatch basically was a festival given by one social unit—the host group—to one or more guest groups, each of which was a recognized societal entity. The host group displayed certain of its traditional hereditary possessions (often called "privileges" in the literature), which might include dances, songs, carvings, and so on, reciting the legends of the origins of these rights and the histories of their recent transmission; presented certain of its members as entitled to use those privileges; bestowed on each of them a new name from the group's hereditary stock (the names were associated with specific levels in social rank, and the higher ranked ones are often compared to titles of nobility in European society); and ended by distributing gifts to the guests. The guests thus were considered to be formal witnesses to the claims of the persons thus presented—that is, the rights to the privileges displayed, to the names bestowed, and to the associated social statuses.

The whole procedure, as Barnett (1938) made clear, had as its purpose the identification of an individual as a member of a certain social unit and the defining of his social position within that unit. Barnett also stressed that, although in descriptive accounts persons of high rank seem to be given all the attention, actually the less fortunate were also identified with their social group by participating as minor dancers, attendants, and singers; as recipients of less important names, which, nonetheless, were part of the group heritage; and as recipients of minor attentions, such as ear and nose piercing and so on. In fine, it is clear that the potlatch must be regarded as a formal procedure for social integration, its prime purpose being to identify publicly the membership of the group and to define the social status of this membership. Barnett has pointed out, as well, that this

A Rare Photograph of a Potlatch at Alert Bay, circa 1900
(Courtesy of Dr. S. W. A. Gunn)

process worked both ways; for the host group not only presented its members but also, in the distribution of gifts, very carefully observed the order of precedence of the guests and used honorific names in addressing them, thus formally recognizing the social order previously claimed by the guests on occasions when they had acted as hosts in such proceedings. This was the essence of the potlatch among all the Northwest Coast groups observing the custom. It will be our purpose to demonstrate that the Southern Kwakiutl did not differ from their neighbors in any important respect.

Southern Kwakiutl Society

Boas' accounts make clear the formal structure of Kwakiutl society. The basic units were local groups which were simultaneously kin groups, that is, made up of persons who were or who considered themselves to be related. The name for such a group in the native idiom Boas wrote as "numaym" (Drucker consistently heard the word as "nàmīmà"). Mr. Nowell insisted that the term means "brothers" ("siblings" would be more precise), without regard to the seniority principle which is stressed in everyday kinship usage. Codere (1961:442) gives Boas' translation "of one kind," from which Mr. Nowell's connotative interpretation seems to derive easily enough. The kinship principle involved in the organization of these groups was bilateral, though with a slight patrilineal bias. A person's major ties were normally felt to be with his paternal kin, but he often associated with, and at least temporarily identified himself with, his maternal relatives. Each namima (this simplified spelling will be used hereafter) possessed lands (fishing places and other sites of economic importance); ceremonial privileges such as names, songs, dances, carvings, and the like; and a set of traditions that included a mythical account of the origin of the family line, mythical and some probably factual adventures of various ancestors usually relating the way in which the family privileges were acquired, and more or less factual accounts of the sources of recently acquired privileges.

The members of each namima were not equals but were graded in a precisely scaled order of precedence. It is usually said that the basis of this ranking was primogeniture, that is, degree of kinship to the direct line of descent from the traditional family ancestor. However, a qualification to this must be noted. Whereas traditional genealogies derive the second, third, and fourth ranking places, and so on, from ancient branches of the line of highest rank (that is, horizontally), the primogeniture principle that operated to designate the highest ranking chief of each namima applied vertically to these lesser ranks in any generation. That is, there was a distinction between potential succession and formal position. Ideally, the eldest son of a line of eldest sons was the ranking chief. His younger brothers were his potential heirs, their right to inherit depending on order of birth in the event that he died without issue. As potential heirs, they were a sort of nobility, entitled to respect, but which held no formal statuses except in exceptional cases. That is, the highest chief's next younger brother was not second chief in formal rank in the group (unless some very special circumstances intervened). The person who held the second formally ranked place had inherited his position through primogeniture from his predecessor, and the same applied to all the other formally titled chiefs. The fact that the namima was a kinship unit meant that all these statuses were tied together genealogically in the family traditions, but once each place had been created for some junior kinsman of the then chief, back in antiquity, the inheritance of that place followed its own direct descent line or the nearest possible equivalent of such direct descent.

The Southern Kwakiutl term for chief is "gialaxa" (first to come down), referring to the fact that the original namima ancestor was believed to have descended to earth in the guise of some supernatural being, such as thunderbird, hawk, or other mythical or animal form, and removed his mask and costume to assume human form. The numerical designators, "second chief," "third chief," and so on, that are occasionally used in English for convenient reference had no counterparts in the formal titles of the chiefs. This sequential ordering was expressed in the order in which the incumbents of these statuses were given their gifts when they were guests at a potlatch, and in the order in which they were called forth to be seated at special places of honor at feasts.

The position of chief among the Southern Kwakiutl, as elsewhere on the Northwest Coast, was regarded by the Indians themselves as one of weighty responsibility. The various properties, economic and ceremonial, really belonged to the basic social group; the ranking chief was the administrator of the family heritage, and the chiefs junior to him were his advisors.

He had to decide when the group should move to their salmon fishing grounds, when their version of the First Salmon rite should be held to ensure a bountiful season's catch, when to begin to exploit the berrying grounds, and the like; and he had to carry out a variety of rituals of economic significance in native opinion. His participation in the potlatch and the feasts was considered as a duty rather than a privilege, an onerous task not to be taken lightly. He was not an arbitrary authoritarian in his dealings with those of his group of lesser rank; after all, even the lowest commoner of the namima was a kinsman and thus entitled to consideration.

Often a number of geographically contiguous namimas (the proper plural in Kwakiutl is nanámīmà) united to form what may be designated as a tribe. The members of such a tribe assembled at a common winter village site; and the constituent basic groups, the namimas, were ranked relative to each other— that is, in a fixed series of precedence which, like that of the individual chiefs within each namima, was recognized in the order in which they were given gifts at potlatches. Thus these tribal organizations may be regarded as essentially ceremonial, that is, for feasts and potlatches; for the local groups gave up little or none of their economic and political independence.

Some groups of tribes which occupied adjoining tracts united into confederacies. Here, as in the tribal organizations, the main symbol of unity was the ranking of the component groups into a single precedence series for the purposes of the potlatch. Although these larger entities—such as the Kwagyuł, who assembled at Beaver Harbor, the site of Fort Rupert, and the Kingcome Inlet groups—achieved their formal structure in the historic period, it is clear that, because of their geographic proximity, the units composing each of the confederacies certainly had had more intimate bonds among themselves for a longer time than with more distant neighbors.

Influences of the Historic Period

When Boas first visited the Southern Kwakiutl at Fort Rupert, they seemed to be a completely wild and savage people, living a thoroughly "primitive" sort of life. Of course Boas was quite aware that they were nothing of the sort. They were a people who had had nearly a century of direct contact with whites; they were familiar with traders, missionaries, British warships, and, more recently, Indian agents. For some years they had been making frequent trips to Victoria and the Fraser River salmon canneries to work for wages. Their consumption of trade goods and dependence on such imports was substantial. Certain of Boas' comments on the condition of Indians at Victoria and his defense of their potlatch, both of which Codere cites,[7] make it obvious that he saw clearly that they were being subjected to enormous and deleterious pressures. These points, however, he did not introduce into his ethnographic descriptions.

Codere's carefully documented analyses (1950, 1961) of Kwakiutl adjustment to the "new economic conditions" demonstrate the transition from membership in an aboriginal surplus-producing economy to a successful participation in the modern cash economy. As she makes clear, this adaptation must be understood to comprehend the potlatch as described by Boas and in its later phases, because the potlatch, although a socio-ceremonial phenomenon, operated with economic materials—that is, wealth goods. It would be pointless to duplicate her data. What we shall do is offer a few supplementary comments and then proceed to note certain other factors affecting Southern Kwakiutl life, especially their potlatching.

An aspect of the transition from an aboriginal to a modern economy that Codere manifestly understands but perhaps might

[7] Codere, 1950:9 and 69, n. 4.

have emphasized more strongly is that Southern Kwakiutl life and the potlatch were enriched by the vast stream of, to them, cheap consumer goods acquired through trade channels. This she demonstrates in her tabulations of valuables distributed in a succession of precontact and historic potlatches (1950:90–93, tables 16, 17); and in regard to the substitution of the woolen trade blanket for native woven and fur robes, she goes on to say, "The result, however, was an almost patent illustration of Gresham's law: the cheaper, more numerous woolen blankets drove out the dearer, and scarcer [aboriginal] blankets" (1950: 95). Since we intend to enlarge on this matter of the "expansion" of the potlatch, it seems worthwhile to note why trade blankets and other trade goods should have been "cheaper." The reason is that aboriginal wealth items were limited in quantity. They were scarcity items, some because of production methods, some for other reasons. A woman weaving a yellow cedar bark robe, with or without mountain-goat wool wefts, did not work at it full time. The robe might be months in the making, beginning with the gathering and preparation of the bark. The weaver worked at it when she was not preparing meals, tending the babies, collecting firewood, and doing other housewifely chores. Canoes, listed by Codere, albeit dubiously, among the miscellany of trifles or "bad things," but formerly, according to Mr. Nowell, major and important potlatch items, similarly took a long time to construct. The canoe maker normally worked alone, and he did not work from sun to sun. Fur robes, mentioned in traditions as prehistoric potlatch goods, had another defect, that of perishability; they were made of raw (untanned) peltries stretched, dried, and sewn together, so that prolonged storage of great quantities of them was impossible. The wool blankets got moth eaten too, but did not deteriorate as rapidly as raw furs in the humid climate. Aboriginal trade items, such as dentalia from Nootkan sources and the famous coppers[8] from the

---

[8] A copper is a large shield-shaped piece, usually with a raised T-shaped ridge in the lower half. Some were incised and painted. Examples collected in the nineteenth century measure about three feet in length. A widely held theory was that the original form was similar but very much smaller and was made of native copper secured by trade from the Athabascan-

north, were likewise in limited supply, because the prevailing condition of intergroup hostility along the coast hampered native commerce, and there was nothing in this region comparable to the great trade mart of the Nass olachon grounds.

On the other hand, the intrusive white civilization offered its goods for things that were relatively abundant. The furbearer population in the region was large, perhaps because it had never been heavily exploited in former times. Commercial salmon fishing came to acquire the same pattern, for salmon abounded (the early salmon fishing on the Fraser was wage work, but the pattern of paying for the fish by weight, and then by the piece, soon developed). Other late nineteenth-century sources of income, such as the sale of dogfish oil and the fur-sealing voyages —at first off Vancouver Island and then to the Bering Sea—likewise came easily. Most of the means for acquiring wealth proffered by the new economy were in fields of native competence. Trapping of land fur, if not intensively practiced anciently, was a familiar skill. The main change eventually introduced, from the old deadfalls to steel traps, was not a great one. Sea hunting, first for sea otter and later for fur seal, was a Southern Kwakiutl specialty; the fur-sealing schooners used to take Kwakiutl or Nootkan hunters, with their own canoes and sealing harpoons, out to intercept the migrating herds. Modern commercial salmon fishing is a complex operation, involving the use of gasoline or diesel engines, heavy gear with power winches, compasses, charts, and tide tables. But early fishing was technologically simple, being done by setting gill nets from skiffs or hauling beach seines at river mouths. If these precise techniques were unknown aboriginally, they were obvious and easy to learn for a people to whom fishing was a prime focus of interest. As a

---

speaking Ahtena of the Copper River. This view has been effectively refuted by Keithahn (1964) who shows that coppers are first mentioned by Europeans on the Northwest Coast in 1804, and that commercial copper plate (carried on ships for sheathing the bottoms) was first introduced to the Northwest Coast tribes by the Spaniards in 1774 and was a desirable trade item for several decades afterward. Keithahn has made a census of coppers and has located 135 in American and European museums. None, so far as can be determined, are made of native copper, and all are made of rolled copper which has not been flattened by hammering.

matter of fact, it was related that the first cannery in Kwakiutl territory, a small operation at Alert Bay, simply bought fish caught by the Indians in their ancient and traditional ways employing traps or harpoons. The gist of all this is that the new economy not only made wealth goods available in abundance to the Kwakiutl, but also provided means to acquire those goods that were both familiar and easy to him, in that way making the trade goods cheap.

A minor aspect perhaps, but one of some interest, is mentioned on several occasions by both Mr. Nowell and Mr. Whonnuck in connection with the greater prosperity long enjoyed by the members of tthe Kwagyuł confederacy deriving from their situation at the site of the trading post. It brings out two points: first, a certain expectable differential among Indian groups in intensities of culture contact in early phases and, second, the acumen of the Kwakiutl in economic dealings where their interest was aroused. It was related that the Fort Rupert groups took to themselves the function of middlemen in the fur trade, visiting remoter groups, not only of Kwakiutl but the Northern Nootkans, to obtain furs which they brought in for sale at the fort—of course, at a substantial profit. Codere (1961:455, and passim) stresses the effects of this pattern. They did so well at this commerce that many chiefs came to devote less time to the fall fishing, and instead bought a considerable part of the winter's supply of dried salmon from their Nimkish neighbors. The zeal for profit led them at times to raiding. Several major raids aimed specifically at looting were made against Northern Nootkans, and one tale was recounted of a large-scale operation against the Bella Coola in which a large force crossed via a trail from the head of Knight Inlet—an arduous and even dangerous journey that involved crossing a glacier and took seven days' travel each way. This expedition staged a successful night attack on an important Bella Coola village, and returned home, it is said, with a treasure trove of furs and other valuables.

As the furbearer population of the region gradually decreased, the Fort Rupert groups (because, said the informants, of their greater familiarity with white men, and also because of the fact that the fort was the only regular port of call for the Hudson's

Bay Company steamer) were the first of the Kwakiutl to go to Victoria to work for wages. Fort Rupert apparently became something of a recruiting center, and it was there, about 1880 or 1881, that the first group, some forty young men, were persuaded to go to the Fraser River salmon fishery. Not all, but most of this group, was said to have been Kwagyuɫ. They had a successful season with steady work at what were considered good wages; so the following year a much larger group, not only from Fort Rupert but from other tribes as well, went to the Fraser. "The Fort Ruperts were always the leaders in dealing with white men," said Mr. Nowell.

There are several other aspects of the culture contact situation besides the changing economic pattern that need to be discussed. Codere has touched on most of them; however, we have additional data on some points and different interpretations to present on others.

The first intimation the Southern Kwakiutl and their neighbors on the British coast had that white civilization was to exert certain regulatory and even inhibitory influence on the native way of life was when they learned that the British government would take severe punitive measures against those who committed serious offenses against white men and, as well, against participants in warfare among the Indians themselves.[9] The matter is important since it represents the Indians' first confrontation with implacable and invincible authority. It was the more significant because warfare to the Southern Kwakiutl, as to their neighbors on the coast, was a highly important activity—prowess in war had a very high rating in their value system.

In developing the theme that the Southern Kwakiutl potlatch was an emotional and social substitute for war,[10] Codere argues that those people were not really warlike, differing in that respect from their neighbors on the coast. She does emphasize that they made a great-to-do about warfare—dramatized it vastly,

[9] Codere, 1950:144 ff., summarizes several such incidents.
[10] This view is accepted by Allen (1956) who proposes other cultural uses of the potlatch and concludes that the basic function of the potlatch was "restoration of social equilibrium."

stressed "atrociousness" as one of their ideals—but her conclusion is that they talked a much better war than they fought. For present purposes, that is in regard to the acculturational effect of the enforced Pax Britannica, it might possibly be enough to accept her interpretation that Kwakiutl war was highly valued culturally even if nearly nonexistent; but it seems preferable, and in the long run adds weight to our argument, to point out that our evidence makes clear that the Southern Kwakiutl shared fully in the war complex typical of their area and were just as warlike as their Nootkan, Heiltsuk, Tsimshian, and other neighbors and perhaps a little more warlike than most Coast Salish groups.

One facet of the difference in opinion seems to stem from Codere's personal definition of "warfare" and "warlike." She regards stress on personal valor as primary in being "warlike," and considers that warfare should consist of two equally armed and matched heroes or groups of heroes meeting on even terms in fair combat. The Southern Kwakiutl were not warlike in her view, because among other things they rarely if ever made an open frontal attack on a foe defensively situated in their well-built winter dwellings. It must be pointed out, however, that such an attack, with an armament of bows and arrows, slings, spears, clubs, and even trade muskets was the epitome of futility; hence the Kwakiutl, like all their warlike neighbors, relied on the surprise attack, particularly at night. The whole matter can be cleared up by adding the adjective "effective" to "warfare." Effective warfare can be defined as the exploitation of any advantage—in manpower, firepower, timing, mobility, and the like—to inflict damage on the enemy. It has been more succinctly defined as "getting thar fustest with the mostest." Effective warfare has very little relationship to the fancies of the romantic poets; the "Charge of the Light Brigade" was not effective warfare. Effective warfare was Hitler's panzer divisions slashing through, cutting off, and chewing up brave but bewildered foes; effective warfare was General Patton doing the same thing—but better—with superiority in manpower, firepower, better equipment, and dominant tactical air support. Effective warfare was the sneak attack on Pearl Harbor, and it was also the Marianas Turkey Shoot, and the Hiroshima bomb. This does not mean that personal bravery does not have a part in effective warfare, but simply that personal bravery is not the *only* necessary ingredient. If this appraisal sounds brutal, that is as it should be, because war is brutal. A certain General Sherman summed it up in three words.

By this definition, the Southern Kwakiutl were warlike and conducted effective warfare. They killed their enemies whenever they outnumbered them, caught them asleep, or otherwise found them at a disadvantage, not waiting until the enemy was in a position to shoot first. All their neighbors, from Tlingit to Nootka and many Coast Salish, conducted warfare in the same way.

Some negative features of Kwakiutl warfare noted by Codere (1950:107) as proof of its inconsequential nature must be reviewed. One was that Kwakiutl wars were not national. Neither were those of any other Northwest Coast group. The nearest thing to national warfare was the traditional war of the nine Coast Tsimshian tribes who settled eventually on Metlakatla Pass against the Tlingit groups said to have been living at the mouth of the Skeena; and even this war, or series of wars, is described as having been waged in piecemeal fashion, as tribal and even clan operations. Another point Codere makes is that Kwakiutl wars had no significant element of economic motivation. This statement can be challenged. The Koskimo originally lived near the Niwiti, near Cape Scott, at a place called qlo'osay (Shuttleworth Bay). They began to wage war on a Kwakiutl-speaking group known as the Hoyaalis (xoya'alis) of Quatsino Sound and finally exterminated them in a series of ruthless surprise attacks, all for the purpose of taking possession of the xoya'alis territory; the victors moved in and have lived there ever since. No date can be estimated for this event, but the tradition is apparently well known among the Southern Kwakiutl. It was recounted to Drucker in some detail by Quatsino Sam in 1937, and referred to by Mr. Nowell in 1953. Again, the Lekwiltok are known to have been fighting their way southeastward into Salish territory; they cannot be dismissed as aberrant just because there are a few more records of their warlike behavior. Finally, the concept that not only material wealth and slaves could be captured in war but even ceremonial prerogatives, which if not in the same class as robes and canoes were enormously valued possessions, indicates that looting did offer a certain incentive to war, thereby adding to the economic factors.[11]

The fact that the Southern Kwakiutl, like all their neighbors on the coast, abandoned their customary warfare in a relatively short time, after a few "incidents" involving confrontation with white authority in the form of British naval units is one of the factors convincing Codere that these people were not really warlike. Other native American groups, those of the Plains for example, resisted much longer. The significant difference, however, was embodied in two interrelated facts: First, Northwest Coast villages, the houses filled with the winter's supplies and tools and gear and the canoes drawn up along the village beach, were immensely vulnerable to naval artillery; and second, the Indians very promptly made a realistic appraisal of their situation in this respect.

We should like to point out here that the ability to evaluate their position vis-à-vis white civilization seems to have been one characteristic of the acculturation of Northwest Coast groups in general. A very careful analysis of this hypothesis should offer some insight into comparative acculturational developments in other areas. The native of other areas undergoing the effects of intensive acculturation, at least as he is usually depicted in the literature, is like a person whose first knowledge of cement mixers occurs through falling into one; he takes a terrible beating without ever quite understanding what is happening to him. The Northwest Coast Indian, on the contrary, seems to have

---

[11] The rather strange (to us) concept that ceremonial rights could be captured in war has been documented by Boas (1897) and Drucker (1951) for Southern Kwakiutl and Nootkans, respectively. It was also a Heiltsuk practice. The procedure of such "capture" involved taking as loot the paraphernalia—masks and the like—and compelling a captive to teach the captors the names, songs, dances, and other procedures. The Nootkans used a special term for privileges obtained in this manner, distinguishing them from privileges obtained through inheritance or in marriage.

comprehended his situation fairly realistically. We suggest that this ability to make rational appraisal, whatever may have been its base, accounts for the following facts among others: There were no large scale wars or uprisings against the white, although the native groups were numerous and warlike;[12] despite all the problems and frustrations, no nativistic cult—that typical flight from acculturative reality—developed or got a foothold on the northern coasts (the Shaker Church of Puget Sound and regions to the south and east must be put in a very special category of "nativistic movements," if indeed it can properly be classified as a nativistic movement at all[13]). Finally, resistance to pressures of white culture took two principal forms: the attempts to use the resistance techniques of white culture and skillfully designed circumvention. The first form refers, among other devices, to the early and continued use by the Indians of white legalistic methods, such as formal petitions to governmental authority, attempts to get relief through use of courts of law, and the like. That many such attempts were inspired by non-Indian friends does not really matter; what is important is that the Indians saw the merit in such advice. The western Apache and Yavapai probably occasionally got some good sound advice in the days before General Crook lowered the boom on them, but they paid no attention to sage counsel. The second method, skillful circumvention, had many manifestations. In one sense, the story we are about to tell of the historic development of the Southern Kwakiutl potlatch is such a case, an instance of highly successful resistance to white authority and law.

To return to our consideration of Kwakiutl warfare and its cessation after brief demonstration of white military superiority, this confrontation not only inhibited the warfare complex and

---

[12] The successful Tlingit uprisings against the Russian posts at Sitka and Yakutat are not exceptions precisely, because they were successful, representing correct evaluations of the military situation. The 1855 attempt at Sitka was so nearly successful also that it barely can be treated as an exception.

[13] Cf. Voget, 1956. The acculturational situation in the Puget Sound region differed markedly from that on the northern coasts (except "Lower Vancouver Island" and the lower Fraser region), for one reason because of the influx of white settlers and dispossession of the Indians.

forced acceptance of alien rule, but had some other effects as well. One was that it permitted frequent contact between groups that formerly met but rarely in peaceful circumstances, both among the Southern Kwakiutl themselves and with their neighbors of other linguistic divisions. Intertribal trade was stimulated, and there was a certain acceleration in the diffusion of traits and complexes of native culture. For example, although the Heiltsuk had long been a source for various features of Winter Dance rites, a great number of ceremonial features were acquired by the Southern Kwakiutl in the closing decades of the nineteenth century as a result of greater familiarity and more frequent intermarriage. However, such effects were side issues, so to speak. As it affected native attitudes toward the acculturational situation, the important aspect of the prohibition of native warfare was that the Indians were made to recognize for the first time the existence of an overwhelmingly superior force that could at will interfere with the native way of life.

In another phase of contact with white culture, that of missionization, the Southern Kwakiutl proved more resistant than many of their coastal neighbors. It is recorded that there was a relatively early, but unsuccessful, effort at conversion by the Roman Catholic Church. Later, the Anglican Church established a mission at Alert Bay. This mission achieved no spectacular immediate results but on a long-term basis has become an important force for cultural change. In part this influence stemmed from the establishment, as part of the missionary effort, of a residential school at Alert Bay at which several generations of Southern Kwakiutl, and for a time Heiltsuk as well, were educated. (In 1953 this school was being operated by the Department of Indian Affairs, to which it had been turned over by the missionary organization.) The Anglican policy appears to have been consistently moderate in its stand on "native custom," in informants' opinions. Mr. Nowell maintained that, although the missionaries vigorously denounced the Shamans' Society performances (the Winter Dances), the potlatch when given separately was opposed not as "heathenish" or non-Christian, but simply because participation was in violation of the law (following passage of an act prohibiting potlatching). The appraisal may be nearly correct, for as the mission's opposition to the potlatch was mild, its effect on that institution seems to have been slight. Many Indians who were regarded as staunch converts continued their participation in the potlatch. This was rather different from the position taken by another Christian sect, the Pentecostal or "Apostolic" Church (as it is often referred to locally), which was introduced in the 1920's. This mission for a time held the interest of a large segment of the Southern Kwakiutl populace. Its view as expressed by its missionaries was very strongly opposed to all aspects of ancient custom, particularly the potlatch. As a consequence various of its converts formally quit the potlatch, abandoning their titles, potlatch places, privileges, and some of them certain related financial obligations.

Discussion of changes in Southern Kwakiutl culture during the historic period would not be complete without mention of the decline in population during this time. Codere (1950:49–61) quite properly discusses this topic at some length, presenting both available population statistics and information as to major factors in population shrinkage, among which imported diseases clearly occupied a significant place. A factor which she does not stress was the large amounts of alcoholic beverages brought from Victoria and Vancouver by free-lance traders and by the Indians themselves, which were the direct cause of a tragically long series of fatalities, chiefly drownings. These unhappy accompaniments of the introduction of white civilization were not, of course, unique to the Southern Kwakiutl; the significant thing here is the meaning of population decline to this native society and to the potlatch.

It has been stated that the personnel comprising each basic social unit—a group of kin, simultaneously a local group, called the namima—were ranked on the basis of genealogical distance from the direct ancestral line in a fixed series from high to low. The ranking of these hereditary social positions was given overt expression by the public assignment of certain names and other privileges from the namima heritage. The names and other prerogatives derived from incidents in the family origin tradition and had fixed associations of rank. That is, name A was to be bestowed on the highest ranking member of the particular namima, name *B* on the person second to him in hereditary status in that group, and so on down the line, although the associations of specific rank with names of low status was less precise. In each namima a certain number of names were considered important enough for their bearers to be accorded special recognition in the potlatch; that is, the persons were given gifts in a sequence corresponding to their ranks when their group was in a guest status at one of these affairs. The bearers of these names were also those entitled, or in the Indian view obliged, to give potlatches or to assist the giver of the potlatch in various formal ways. In brief, these were the occupants of the "potlatch places," the individuals referred to by the term translated into English as "chief." To the Indians it was essential that the series of potlatch places was complete. Decline of population meant that more and more frequently there were no survivors in degree of kinship regarded as properly close to the ideal direct line—son, or younger brother, or even a younger brother's son—when the incumbent of a high status died or, as often was done, when an incumbent of such a position wishes to bestow his name and privileges on an heir, in effect retiring.

Miss Codere (1950:97) notes that according to Boas' count there were "at least 658 potlatch positions in the Kwakiutl social system," that is, the combined totals of all the tribes. She also notes that by 1898, the first year in which the record gives a breakdown on population composition, there were only 637 males sixteen years or more of age; in other words, there were 21 more potlatch places than men to occupy them. This imbalance became more and more pronounced as the population continued to dwindle until it reached its all-time low in 1924 (Codere, 1950:57). Codere implies that the solution was to distribute the places all around, so that eventually all the Southern Kwakiutl were chiefs. In actual fact the problem did not work out as simply as that. Apparently fairly early in the phase of population decline, women began to inherit potlatch places, but there was some resistance to the idea of accepting a woman as proper heir to one of the higher ranking statuses. Small children were often formally placed in the statuses, the "retiring" chief continuing to function behind the scenes in a sort of power-behind-the-throne role. Some places were left vacant, despite the feeling against this. Often heirs were sought among distant relatives, at times so distant that the individuals chosen were actually of low rank—not chiefs at all—prior to their acceptance of the heritage. It is especially important that at times easy solutions were not found, and as a result a great many conflicts and stress situations developed. Sometimes two or more persons, about equally distant genealogically from the direct line, desired the place. Occasionally, potentially satisfactory candidates refused to accept a position. One individual might hold several places simultaneously, despite the fact that there was some disapproval of this, and on formal occasions he would fill these places with younger distant kin, who served, as it were, as proxies. Adoption was resorted to at times. For example, Boas' interpreter and informant, George Hunt, the son of the Scottish factor at the Hudson's Bay Company post at Fort Rupert and of a Tsimshian woman, who grew up among the Kwagyuł, came to hold a chief's name and status and carried out all the associated duties of his formal position—functioning in the potlatch and dancing as a Hamatsa in the Shamans' Society performances—because he was adopted by the hereditary holder of those rights. One of our informants, Mr. Whonnuck, was kwagyuł on his father's side; his mother was walas kwagyuł and nimqic. He inherited a chief's place of lower rank among the kwagyuł from his father, in addition to certain rights acquired by his father in marriage, and an Eagle position from his mother (which had not been given to his father in the marriage transactions). He also held the name q!wumxilagilis and its associated prerogatives in the ninulqenux namima of the nimqic, rights that he inherited from his mother's mother's brother.

A lengthy series of similar examples could be cited, but the foregoing should make clear that by the latter part of the nineteenth century the Southern Kwakiutl were going to extreme lengths to try to hold together what they regarded as the most important part of their social structure: The potlatch itself was of abiding interest to the Southern Kwakiutl, but they were willing to admit changes in its procedure and in certain of its other aspects, some of which we shall document in subsequent pages. What they did not do willingly was to permit changes in their system of formal social rank, which it was the basic function of the potlatch to define. We note in passing that this is one of the few points where our interpretation of significant changes in the contact period differs sharply from Codere's. She takes the position that, during what she calls the "Potlatch Period" (1849-1921), potlatching was done for its own sake, "Crests," she states, "became less important than the property distributions that validated them" (1961:467). Our informants invariably stressed the fact that the validation of the "crests" (privileges, in our usage), that is, the system of formal rank, was always the prime motive in potlatching, even during the epoch of the most spectacular wealth distributions, Codere's "Potlatch Period."

One of the few fortunate circumstances in the story of the acculturation of this people was that there was no flood of settlers crowding them out of their ancestral homes. Southern Kwakiutl territory is in general quite unsuitable for agriculture. The prospectors who fought their way along the turbulent streams and up the rocky slopes never found more than a few glints of "color" in their gold pans. Canadian regulations did not permit the developing canned salmon industry to bar the Indian from his fishing places and thus prevented the acute economic problems that confronted the Tlingit and Haida of Alaska. Logging did not become an important activity in Southern Kwakiutl territory, except at Cape Mudge in Lekwiltok country, until about the turn of the century; even then it seems to have been a rather small-scale operation for a number of years, except in Quatsino Sound where a pulp mill was built. Eventually Alert Bay came to be a center of logging operations. Also about the turn of the century, a small colony of Finns was settled at Sointula. It is said they intended to devote themselves to farming and made extensive clearings that fifty years later could scarcely be distinguished from strands of virgin timber.

Of necessity they became fishermen, part-time trappers, and loggers. There had been some conflict with the Indians, some of whom accused the Finns of making a practice of robbing trap lines, but in general it seems that there has been little intergroup contact. All in all, white settlement of Southern Kwakiutl territory has been sparse, certainly in comparison to that of "lower" Vancouver Island and the lower Fraser Valley, so that one may say that there were some acculturative stresses that these Indians were spared.

An Indian agency was established among the Kwakiutl in 1881 with a jurisdiction corresponding fairly closely to linguistic boundaries, continuing the direct administrative pressures initially introduced in the punitive measures taken in the prohibition against native warfare. Indian agents had legal authority to try offenders and award punishments for minor offenses and to bring charges in more serious violations of the law that automatically resulted in the arrest and trial of the accused Indians before provincial courts. There were times in the early days of the confederation of British Columbia with the Dominion when policy conflicts between province and Dominion hampered cooperation and diminished the agent's effectiveness in matters of law enforcement; the agent, of course, was a federal officer and the mechanisms of law enforcement—police, courts, and the like—were provincial instruments. In the long run, however, the agent's disciplinary functions became a potent force in cultural change.

The first direct effect of the coming of Canadian law and order on the institution of the potlatch itself occurred in 1876 when an article expressly prohibiting both the potlatch and Shamans' Society performances (Winter Dances) was written into the Indian Act. The law in a revision of the Indian Act in 1885, read as follows:

> Every Indian or other person who engages in or assists in celebrating the Indian festival known as the "Potlatch" or in the Indian dance known as the "Tamanawas" is guilty of a misdemeanor, and shall be liable to imprisonment for a term not more than six nor less than two months in any gaol or other place of confinement; and any

Indian or other person who encourages, either directly or indirectly, an Indian or Indians to get up such a festival or dance, or to celebrate the same, or who shall assist in the celebration of same, is guilty of a like offense, and shall be liable to the same punishment.

This law was promulgated mainly at the urging of the missionaries and officials concerned with administering Indian affairs, who concurred in regarding the potlatch as the essential hindrance to what they called the Indian's "progress." If we look at the problem from their point of view, it is plain that they were probably correct—if, that is, we accept the assumptions of both agents and missionaries and many other whites of the period as well that the solution to the so-called Indian Problem was to make an imitation white man out of the Indian, preferably an imitation white farmer. Farming somehow had a respectable connotation in white Canadian and American thinking of the Victorian period (perhaps because a farmer was a steady worker who did not make enough money to support any major vice), although since that time there has developed the "Tobacco Road" school which asserts that peasant farming and Victorian morality do not of necessity go hand in hand. In the view of the late nineteenth-century agents and missionaries, it was most promising that the coast Indians had demonstrated a capacity to stand up to the discipline of the day's work by white standards—laboring from sun to sun for the modest daily wage. This was in contrast to the plains Indian (in Canada they said "prairie Indian") who preferred to lie down beside his plow and go sound asleep or else scamper off on his pony to search for the (diminishing) buffalo.

The Coast Indian demonstrated a comprehension of the economic values of the day. But what did he do when he was paid off after his season of industry? Did he spend his hard-won earnings for things regarded as beneficial and progressive by Victorian standards? Did he invest them sagaciously for future benefit? He did not. He blew the works in a "potlatch." Missionaries said, and probably correctly, that he let his children shiver in the cold while he gave away blankets by the bale. He also learned about the "quick buck." A dollar gained by the whoring of his wife, sisters, or daughters was just as acceptable to the white rulers of the new economic world for the purchase of blankets as a dollar gained in a long day of picking hops or hauling gill net on the Fraser. Bootlegging was another easy-money proposition; few Indian canoes departed Victoria that did not sail down to their marks with a cargo of liquor to be resold at their home ports. All these profits went into the potlatch. Since, although they deplored it, neither officials nor missionaries could realistically hope to alter the white man's institutions of vice, they chose as their target the potlatch, in which the Indian expended both his honest and ill-gotten gains.

The enactment of the anti-potlatch law ushered in a lengthy comedy of administrative errors. The first, of course, may be noted in the language of the law itself, which obviously, by its failure to define "Potlatch" and "Tamanawas," set the stage for confusion. This put the onus of defining what the misdemeanor actually consisted of on the courts trying cases in violation. Schooled in the rigid justice of British law, the jurists were put in an impossible position. How could they find, even when a non-English speaking defendant was supposed to be pleading "guilty," to an undefined offense?

Another fatal error of the early potlatch law was its failure to include measures for implementation or to provide them through other (for example, budgetary) legislation. The agents, when they came on the scene, were required to enforce a poorly written law with no police assistance, no physical means of effective enforcement.

The language of the law was eventually revised to put more teeth into it. And in time arrangements were made for assigning a police officer to each agency to assist the agent in law enforcement, and provincial courts were able to cooperate. La Violette (1961:44–97) has summarized the events in this sequence of change from the original administrative frustration to the more effective, but never completely effective, inhibitory action. His summary, magnificently documented but weak in ethnographic appraisal, indicates that the anti-potlatch law was inconsequential in effect until about 1920. This is not quite so, if our informants are to be believed. They insisted that most of the agents repressed the potlatch with all the force they could demand. Some tended to be tolerant in the early phase of their administrations but invariably came to fight the institution, through the media of threats, control of movement of the Indians, and the like.

When, early in the present century, Royal Canadian Mounted Police (or provincial police) were assigned to the agency by provincial authorities, their principal activities related to suppressing the liquor traffic and the potlatch. Legally or extralegally, the agents prohibited assemblages of Indians, forced certain groups to reside at Alert Bay (the site of the agency), and allowed them to depart individually or in groups only with the agent's permission. The evolution of that apparent contradiction in terms, "the secret potlatch," derived from suppressive efforts by the Indian agents, who exerted all manner of persuasion, threats, and force, according to Mr. Nowell and Mr. Whonnuck. At the same time, to be fair in our appraisals of the situation, we must recognize that the agents of the Kwakwalla Agency were hardworked, underpaid, conscientious civil servants trying to do their duty under impossible conditions. They were, as the Spanish proverb has it, "between the sword and the wall." They were made responsible for enforcing an unenforceable law. Whatever they did was wrong. If they did not try to enforce the law, there were numerous witnesses, especially missionaries, to accuse them of being derelict in their duties. If they tried to enforce it, they were still wrong. A case remanded for trial that did not obtain a conviction owing to the faulty language of the law not only affected the agent's prestige among his charges but might well bring him a reprimand from his superiors.

When at long last the law was rewritten in more intelligible language (the Indian Department in Ottawa insisted on retaining the law) so that Agent Halliday eventually could get convictions of offenders, an enormous protest by self-styled "friends of the Indians" was heard. La Violette (1961:66 ff.) sketches the development of a vociferous antiagent, propotlatch group of writers of letters to the editor, letters to members of Parliament, and the like. Most of this group cannot be identified to determine what they actually knew about the Indians and the potlatch. A few can be. La Violette notes Boas' letter, published in the *Province*, and states that the letter was apparently intended to be private and was published by the recipient. He also notes a letter from Chief Maquinna of Nootka Sound. Now, after all, we all know that Professor Boas was literate; but that particular Chief Maquinna, we know, was not literate and spoke almost no English. It would be interesting to know who put all those elegant words in his mouth. Letters and petitions from other illiterate, non-English-speaking Indians include similar handsome diction. This is something La Violette clearly sensed but could not define in his study, for the data are not to be found to explain the real raison d'être for the interest group of whites who opposed even such partial application of the anti-potlatch law as could be carried out.

In summary, a law prohibiting potlatching was promulgated but could not be enforced for various reasons. The various agents among the Kwakiutl tried to enforce the law and could not, but were nonetheless able to exert enough pressure so that the Indians had to modify their potlatch drastically in order to keep it at all. What is significant here is the pattern of such changes.

By the turn of the century it seems to have been considered by whites and Indians alike on the coast that this law was aimed specifically at the Southern Kwakiutl, although that had not originally been the case. Neighbors to the northward, Tsimshian, Niska, Haida, and even some of the Heiltsuk had under missionary influence given up the macabre Dancing Society performances (those involving cannibalistic representations and mutilation had never attained importance among most Tsimshian-speaking groups or the Haida) and had so modified their potlatches, where they had not given them up altogether like Duncan's Metlakatlans, that neither missionaries nor agents objected to them. The Nootkans, almost inaccessible in that day, especially during the winter season of potlatching, and familiar only to a few hard-bitten cannery men and a very few missionaries, shocked no white sensibilities with their Wolf Dance version of the Shamans' Society performance. But the missionary-resistant Southern Kwakiutl enthusiastically continued their "heathen" practices, not only giving away but also destroying valuables and money. And, in connection with many potlatches, their Cannibal Dancers (Hamatsa) bit flesh from the arms of their fellows in a horribly gory fashion, and gormandized on human corpses in what must have been—whether the corpses were real or just exceedingly realistic stage props—one of the world's more appalling forms of public entertainment.[14]

The agents were never able to stop the potlatches. In the early years of their attempts, that is, immediately following the enactment of the law when Dominion-Provincial cooperation was at low ebb, they could not get provincial courts to convict violators of the anti-potlatch law. Later, after that situation had improved, other difficulties appeared. There was only one agent at a time and one policeman assigned to the agency; the Southern Kwakiutl, although sadly reduced in numbers, were still many and widely scattered. One of the early agents devised a partial solution: he compelled the Kwagyuł and some of the other worst offenders to come to live at Alert Bay, where the agency was situated and he could keep an eye on them. The housing situation became acute, and subsistence problems arose. He had to give the outsiders permission, at times, to return to their home territories to fish, hunt, and pick berries. He must have known that every time they got out of his sight they gave potlatches, even out of the normal season for such affairs. The Kingcome Inlet tribes apparently were never held at the agency; there were too many of them and they were too far from their sources of supply. They began to winter in one of their villages above the mouth of the river, which froze over in wintertime. There in their frosty isolation they potlatched as much as they pleased.

Despite the handicaps under which the agents operated, they

[14] There are grounds for doubting that real human corpses were ever actually used, or, if used, actually devoured, that need not be gone into here. Curtis (1915) lists some of them. The point here is that, whether real or theatrical make-believe, the performances rarely failed to shock and horrify white spectators.

made potlatching difficult. Indians were arrested, jailed, and fined and their potlatch gear—masks, costumes, coppers—was confiscated. Changes were forced in potlatch procedures, and subterfuges had to be devised. On one occasion, it was related, when a new agent had just taken over, a chief planned a flour potlatch at Alert Bay. Great piles of sacks of flour were stacked across the rear end of the house when the agent entered with the policeman. When the agent inquired if a potlatch was being given, he was blandly told it was no such thing—the chief was merely going to distribute Christmas presents to his fellow villagers. The agent was not fooled, of course. He rebuked the chief sharply, although he did not then order his arrest. This particular agent proved to be extremely rigid in his enforcement of the anti-potlatch law.

Now the potlatch was not, to the Kwakiutl, simply an occasion for jollity, feasting, and giving or receiving presents, although it included these elements. Nor was it, as Benedict asserted, a mechanism for relieving tensions derived from psychic abnormalities or for making such abnormalities normal, if one wishes to look at her thesis in this way. Rather, the potlatch was the heart of the Southern Kwakiutl social structure, the system of hereditary rank. An Indian might be entitled by birth to a noble name, a name that defined his position in native society as one entitled to honor and respect. Yet he could never use that name or any of the accompanying privileges unless he gave a potlatch at which he testified publicly to his hereditary right to assume it. Even to the low-born man the potlatch was dear, for in his participation, if only in a minor role, he found the security of identification with his group and shared a reflected glimmer of the glory of his chief. Consequently, passage of a law prohibiting the institution and attempts at enforcement by one agent and one dismounted Royal Canadian Mounted Policeman, or even by several agents and several policemen had the budget allowed them, could not stamp out the custom. The introduction of the element of outwitting the agent gave an added zest. It is quite clear that the potlatch became even more esteemed and cherished, acquiring overtones of defiance of the unwelcome authority of the agent, defiance of the laws of white civilization that the Indians felt were closing in on them. In addition, since the complex revolved about the values of ancient heritages—the names and privileges—it acquired a certain nostalgic cast. It thus became at once a symbol of defiance and a reminder of the good old days. Potlatching burgeoned. The Golden Age of Southern Kwakiutl potlatching could justifiably be defined as the period from 1885 to 1952. In 1952 a revised Indian Act was drafted, a version from which the article concerning potlatching had been dropped. After the new act went into effect, when potlatching was once more legal, a mamaleleqala chief invited the Kwagyuł and the nimqic to an olachon—a grease "feast," such a feast essentially being a potlatch at which large numbers of five-gallon cans of grease are given away. Only a scant handful of old men bothered to attend the affair.

Changes in Potlatch Procedures

The purpose of the present section is to assemble data given by the informants concerning changes in the potlatch. Some of these changes were ones that they themselves had observed during their respective lifetimes; their knowledge of others was derived from comments and explanations by their elders, traditional accounts, and the like. It should be noted that most of these points were developed by the informants in general discussions, in clarifying details of procedure, and were not elicited by direct questioning. Certain of the changes will be given only summary mention here, since they are to be discussed in more detail in other connections. In broad terms, two trends can readily be seen in the overall pattern: first, a consistent picture of expansion and increase in complexity of the institution during the period beginning in early historic times until 1952; and second, modifications designed to circumvent administrative pressure, that is, efforts by the agents to enforce the antipotlatch law. The first of these trends corroborates to a high degree one derived by Codere from an analysis of Boas' materials and historical records. Our material is fuller because of its nature, and because the informants certainly understood that the field ethnographer was interested both in the mechanics of the potlatch and in these matters of changes.

Both Mr. Nowell and Mr. Whonnuck averred that they had often heard statements that in olden times, that is, in the prehistoric period, feasts were frequent but potlatches were few and far between. This, it may be noted, was in accord with reports by Drucker's Nootkan informants and makes sense in terms of the relative scarcity of aboriginal potlatch goods in comparison with the abundance of trade goods. This is substantiated by Codere's (1950:90–91) résumé of "forty-four Kwakiutl potlatches (c. 1729–1936)." (However, we seriously question the total absence of trade items in affairs after 1790 and prior to the founding of the post at Fort Rupert. Firearms were highly prized in the early days of trade and, among the Nootkans for instance, were premium items in early historic potlatches.) In any event, we are prepared to accept the informants' statements as reasonable and probably correct.

In those early times only the highest ranking chief in each namima ever gave a potlatch, which helps account for the infrequent occurrence of these affairs in that period. Mr. Nowell qualified this by saying that it was his understanding that on rare occasions a chief second in rank might give a potlatch also. He appeared to be referring to certain instances cited in traditional histories of the sociological fission of a namima into senior and junior branches, as in the kwagyuł (gw'etala) gixsàm, which split after some internal dissension, one branch shifting to become a namima of the walas kwagyuł. The potlatching by the future head of the junior branch, the chief second in rank, was a part of the splintering-off process. In those days the potlatch wealth was assembled through the effort of the entire namima. Chiefs junior to the highest in rank and commoners as well contributed whatever wealth goods they had to their chief in preparation for the potlatch. This pattern of group effort persisted much longer among the Nootkan groups. "Everybody in the namima had to help their chiefs," said Mr. Whonnuck. "It was something like nowadays we have to pay taxes to the government."[15]

It is clear that potlatching only by ranking chiefs was an expression of the relative scarcity of potlatch goods, not an exclusive prerogative; for a few traditional accounts, apparently describing an early period, cite exceptions, although invariably in some special circumstances. Further, there are no references to objections being raised or conflicts created when the chiefs of medium and lower rank began to potlatch. Commoners, however, were not permitted to give potlatches. Just when lesser chiefs began to potlatch is difficult to estimate, except that this

---

[15] Indian salmon fishermen earning their incomes not on their "reserves" but from fishing in territorial waters were at the time of collection of these data liable for payment of Canadian income tax, a fact causing some resentment among them.

was unquestionably correlated with the expanded wealth economy of the Southern Kwakiutl well along in the latter half of the nineteenth century. Codere (1950:97) cities historic records showing that this practice had reached the point where it had become obvious to white observers by the early 1880's. The economic significance is that the financing of the potlatch became an individual not a group enterprise. Cooperation by members of the namima, or in major potlatches by the giver's entire tribe, continued to be rendered in the form of services; the group aided as singers, dancers, attendants, waiters, and fetchers and carriers in general.

Directly related to this change was one concerning the amounts of the gifts. When only the ranking chiefs potlatched, informants stated, the amounts of the gifts distributed directly reflected the order of rank. That is, the ranking chief of each guest namima received not only the first gift given to members of his group but also the largest gifts. His brother chiefs, his juniors in the namima, received successively smaller gifts. Mr. Whonnuck added that he had been told that frequently commoners were not given gifts at all. Instead, the chiefs, and particularly the first chief who had received the principal gift, were expected to redistribute their own gifts, or a considerable share of them among their commoner kin, as continued to be customary with food gifts at feasts—beyond the food actually consumed. The chief receiving such a gift of food called his people to an informal feast on his return home, making a point of including the aged and others who had been unable to attend the feast, redistributed his gift portion among them and recounted the significant events of the affair at which he had received his gift. This informant believed that potlatch gifts were handled anciently in this same manner.

Once potlatching by lesser chiefs came into vogue, however, this method of rating gifts to the guests changed. Sometimes a chief of lower rank had given a major potlatch, whereas some, at least, of his seniors in rank had not. Consequently, when his namima was in a guest status at a potlatch given by one of his former guests, such a man would receive a present larger than those given to some or all of his superiors. Development of this concept obviously created a major change in the economies of giving in the potlatch.

Mr. Whonnuck, for example, gave a flour feast in 1932, at which he distributed one thousand sacks of flour to the Kwagyuł, mamaleleqala, nimqic, ławitsis, ma'amtagila, and Kingcome Inlet tribes. Such affairs were termed "feasts" and followed the feast precedence order of distribution; but in some respects they were like potlatches, for the gifts consisted of entire sacks of flour. A detailed accounting of the distribution was not recorded, but the informant said he gave an average of four to five sacks of flour to most of the chiefs, except that to the very highest ranking chiefs of the tribes he gave six to eight sacks. There was, however, a ma'amtagila chief of medium rank who on a previous occasion had given the informant eight sacks of flour; to him Mr. Whonnuck gave eighteen sacks. A Kingcome Inlet chief who was the only one who had given a feast to the Kwagyuł in recent years was given ten sacks, more than any of his higher ranking colleagues. A mamaleleqala chief who, as a close friend, had given much assistance in the affair—making arrangements to house the guests and the like (the major part of the affair was given at Village Island)—was given ten sacks to indicate appreciation of his special services.

The sort of distribution described above, which took into account both rank and previous potlatching of the guests and even special courtesies, was typical of the Southern Kwakiutl potlatch during and after the closing decades of the nineteenth century. We repeat, to stress the point, that the informants themselves regarded this as a change from the traditional method in which the value of the gift was directly proportional to, and only to, the relative rank of the recipient. The change was an outgrowth of the proliferation of potlatch giving, altering the ancient pattern according to which only the ranking chief gave potlatches under normal circumstances, utilizing contributions made to him by his entire namima in assembling his stock of potlatch goods.

A suggestion not offered by the informants, but one which occurs as a logical possibility, is that the creation of the eagle positions may have set the pattern for the rating of potlatch gifts according to the recipient's previous gift. The origin of the eagle places will be discussed in detail later; we shall note here only that most if not all were quite certainly innovations of the historic period, and the late historic period at that. Since the eagles were not, properly speaking, chiefs, gifts made to them had to be calibrated on the basis of the recipient's previous gift. This concept might well have provided the model for rating the amount of the gift to be made to a minor chief who had given a major potlatch. It seems clear from the evidence that the first two or three of the eagle places were created in the earlier part of the historic period, before potlatching by chiefs of medium and low rank became prevalent.

A significant change in the potlatch, and one which was in one sense part of the "expansion" of the institution, can be defined as the progressive increase of the guest group. Since time immemorial, there had been a limited amount of peaceful contact between all the Southern Kwakiutl tribes, and even with certain of their neighbors—Nootkans (especially the moatcath of Nootka Sound), the nearer Coast Salish, and certain Heiltsuk groups. On the basis of these contacts, rare but never-forgotten intertribal marriages had been arranged, which resulted in the creation of a network of affinal ties among the groups. However, the prevalent hostility pattern prevented the affinal relationships from having much practical significance in leading to greater frequency of peaceful contact. Once the bride price, and then its "repayment," had been transferred on the occasion of a marriage between remotely situated social units, formal contacts between the in-laws were few. They did not continue to meet frequently for feast and potlatch festivals in ancient times. The groups that were in frequent contact—those who were both closely related by frequent intermarriages and who customarily invited each other to feasts and potlatches—were just as one would anticipate on logical grounds those occupying contiguous territories, who at times even held adjoining tracts on fishing grounds and the like. It is easy to see that where intermarriage was common the bilateral principle on which Southern Kwakiutl society was constructed would favor development of closer ties between the groups involved. That it did not do so in intermarriages between remotely situated groups was clearly because of the danger inherent in travel in the days of native warfare. The informants were specific as to the definite limits of what we may term the "festival groups" in former days. Although there was no formal native term for these festival units, they were nevertheless quite real, and their basis was geographic proximity.

In discussing this matter, both Mr. Nowell and Mr. Whonnuck began with the festival group to which their own Kwagyuł confederacy belonged, as was to be expected. The "Fort Ruperts," that is, the three, formerly four, tribes of the Kwagyuł confederacy, potlatched among themselves and with the mamaleleqala, the nimqic, the ławitsis, and the tenaxtɔx of Knight Inlet, the last-named group being a special case, as will be noted. The extinction of the q!omkutis tribe obviously gave the informants some trouble in their efforts to reconstitute for us the ancient system of relationships. Mr. Nowell, in the pairings of the tribes, tentatively suggested the q!omkutis may have been matched with—that is, may have potlatched with—the tenaxtɔx and the ma'amtagila (matilpe). Mr. Whonnuck said he could not recall having heard with whom the q!omkutis had potlatched. There was, it appears, some doubt even in the days of Boas' early work (1897:328–332, 343), for he gives two lists of these same pairings, one of which matches the qòmkutis with the nimqic and the other with the ławitsis. His lists include the qwexsotenɔx (Qoexsot'enox) as the potlatch-mate group of the kwɛna (Q'omoyue), which probably means that this group should have been included in the lists given by Nowell and Whonnuck. For many years, however, the qwexsotenɔx have associated closely with, and potlatched with, the Kingcome Inlet groups and have been considered members of that festival unit. In any case, both informants insisted that all traditions with which they were familiar made clear that anciently the Kwagyuł potlatched with, that is, invited and were invited by, only those tribes mentioned. What the "pairings" seem to mean is that even within the festival group there were once narrower limits, each tribe inviting only the tribe matched with it in the lists, although this is not completely clear. What was brought out specifically and unequivocally in connection with the relative status ratings of the tribes was that formerly only one tribe was invited to a potlatch at a time; it was for this reason that there was no defined tribal precedence order rating for nimqic, mamaleleqala, and ɬawitsis until a series of incidents, to be described in detail later on, occurred.

The Knight's Inlet groups were in a special relationship with the Kwagyuɬ because of the latter's ownership of olachon fishing rights at Knight's Inlet and consequent annual visits there. It was reported that not infrequently one or more Kwagyuɬ namima stayed on through the summer at Knight's Inlet after the olachon run for berry picking and would invite, and be invited by, the Knight's Inlet groups to feasts and minor potlatches. These people were not, however, invited to the major potlatches given in the old tribal villages or at Fort Rupert in olden times. Presumably the major potlatches that the Knight's Inlet groups held in the winter season were given among themselves.

Another festival group was constituted by the niwiti, the naqoaqtɔq, and the goasila. Mr. Nowell speculated that the koskimox may have feasted and potlatched with these groups occasionally, because of the fact that the koskimox had been neighbors of the niwiti before they captured the territories of the xoya'alis in war and moved into Quatsino Sound. Although Quatsino Sam did not present his data in exactly the same way, he indicated that after moving into Quatsino Sound the principal contacts of the koskimox were with their neighbors of the sound; he did not mention the niwiti as close friends. He did make clear that frequent contacts with the Fort Ruperts began comparatively late. If the Quatsino Sound tribes did form a festival unit apart, there was one overlap outside the Sound—the Lǃaskino, whom the Koskimo informant pictured as a group very closely linked to the Nootkan tciklisath through frequent intermarriages and who often visited and were visited by their Nootkan-speaking kin. The koskimox and other groups of the sound did not participate in this interchange with the Nootkans except when individuals related to the Lǃaskino accompanied these last-named.

Another festival unit was constituted by the Kingcome Inlet tribes, who even in more recent times did a great deal of potlatching among themselves. One reason, of course, for this separatist trend was that during the many years of administrative pressure against the potlatch these tribes were almost inaccessible to the agent and the police officer in the winter season. Both Mr. Nowell and Mr. Whonnuck coincided, as was indicated previously, in including the qwexsotenux with the Kingcome Inlet groups, that is, along with the tsawatenux, guauenox, and haxwɔmis. As already noted, this is contradicted by Boas' material, which includes the qwexsotenux in the Kwagyuɬ-mamaleleqala-nimqic-ɬawitsis division. The possibility exists that their affiliation as reported by Boas may have become established in the latter half of the nineteenth century as part of the breakdown of the old festival groupings, so that the more recent association with the Kingcome Inlet divisions would have represented a return to an older pattern.

The lɛkwiɬtɔk (Lekwiltok) divisions constituted another distinct festival unit. They potlatched among themselves and occasionally with Salish neighbors such as the Comox, although informants believed that such crossing of linguistic boundaries probably began after intertribal warfare had been stopped. At any rate, they did not potlatch with other Southern Kwakiutl until the twentieth century.

The informants both noted that they did not know the earlier potlatch affiliations of the ma'amtagila (matilpe). This was a small unit which was supposed to have split off from the ma'amtagila namima of the kwagyuɬ (gwétala), apparently just prior to or at the beginning of early historic times. They resumed contacts with the Kwagyuɬ sometime after the formation of the confederacy at Fort Rupert. Mr. Nowell was of the opinion that this occurred prior to the breakdown of the festival groupings and tentatively suggested that they may have been paired with the q!omkitis, as already mentioned.

This, then, was the intertribal situation among the Southern Kwakiutl in aboriginal times and through the early historic period, persisting apparently for a time even after the establishment of the Hudson's Bay Company post at Fort Rupert. There were at least five distinct groupings of tribes (or six if it is correct that the Knight's Inlet people constituted a separate festival group apart from their spring and summer contacts with the Kwagyuł) who gave feasts and potlatches among themselves, rarely with outsiders. The infrequent exceptions to this practice were the marriages between members of groups of different festival units. The groupings were easily defined geographic blocks, that is, formed by groups whose territories adjoined and who might be expected under normal conditions to have closer contact among themselves than with more distant divisions. It is also indicated that in those days an outstanding potlatch was one to which a single neighbor tribe was invited; more common affairs were the a'wi'sila, "potlatch to one's own tribe," where the chief of one namima invited the other namima of his own tribe.

The first symptom of change in this pattern may with reasonable certainty be attributed to the expanding economy of the Southern Kwakiutl. It occurred when certain chiefs of the Kwagyuł began to invite the nimqic and the mamaleleqala simultaneously, and then the ławitsis as well. These, in their turn, began to invite all the Fort Rupert tribes simultaneously.

It was not possible to give a precise date for the entry of the first outsiders—niwiti, naqoaqtɔq, goasila, and koskimox—into potlatch relationships with the Kwagyuł group. Probably an estimated allocation to the decade 1870–1880 would not be far wrong. It is easier to define the factors making this development possible. One, unquestionably, was the other tribes' increased familiarity with the Kwagyuł as one result of these people's busy trading activities in collecting furs for resale to the Hudson's Bay Company. Another was the establishment of the Pax Britannica that reduced intergroup contacts from perilous adventure to the commonplace. This operated in two ways, broadly speaking. On the one hand, it facilitated peaceful encounters between the Southern Kwakiutl groups concerned. As has been indicated these groups occasionally met peaceably, even in ancient times, but the menace of a surprise assault always made such encounters uneasy. On the other hand, the imposed peace simultaneously increased contacts between niwiti, naqoaqtɔq, and goasila with Heiltsuq and other groups to the north. They began to acquire both articles of native trade and ceremonial privileges through such contacts, thus becoming potential sources of these desirable items from the Kwagyuł point of view, hence worth cultivating. The far-ranging "Sebassas"—the Kitkahtla Tsimshian of Porcher Island—formed the habit of putting in at the niwiti and naqoaqtɔq villages to sell the coppers they brought from the north (their long history of enmity with the Kwagyuł apparently made them unwilling to risk calling at Fort Rupert). The niwiti and naqoaqtɔq thus became important links in the trade in coppers. For these groups, friendly relationships with the Kwagyuł must have had the added attraction of giving easier and more frequent access to the trading post, saving the exorbitant middleman's commission exacted by the Kwagyuł. At any rate, there were significant motivations on both sides toward the intensifying contacts.

Apparently in the late 1880's, Mr. Nowell's elder brother gave what was said to have been the greatest potlatch given up to that time, both in the quantity of wealth distributed and, specifically, in the number of tribes invited. As chief of the kwexa he invited as guests the kwagyuł, walas kwagyuł, mamaleleqala, nimqic, ławitsis, ma'amtagila, niwiti, naqoaqtɔq, and koskimox. Some years later, about 1896 or 1897 as nearly as can be estimated, Mr. Whonnuck's father's father surpassed this feat. He invited *all* the Southern Kwakiutl groups except the Lekwiltok to a potlatch which he gave in the name of his son.

These two high points in potlatch history clearly show the trend toward expansion in guest groups that developed simultaneously with the increase in the amount of wealth distributed. Of course, during this same period other chiefs were giving potlatches to these groups that formerly had been outside of the Kwagyuł festival unit, the difference being that they invited, for example, only Kingcome Inlet divisions, or the koskimox, or the niwiti and naqoaqtɔq, or the goasila, and so on. It was in this way that the intertribal precedence lists—which included all the Southern Kwakiutl—reported by Boas were developed.[16] These pan-Kwakiutl precedence lists certainly did not exist even in native theory a few decades earlier, when the festival groupings were completely exclusive. The customary guests of the Kwagyuł—the nimqic, mamaleleqala, and ławitsis—did not have any defined order of precedence among themselves, because they had never been guests at a potlatch simultaneously. The date at which a precedence order was established among these three tribes is uncertain. However, we believe that the resolution of this problem occurred well after the establishment of the Hudson's Bay Company post, for one thing because the chiefs of the Kwagyuł confederacy, who resolved the matter, acted with a unanimity that suggests they had become accustomed to close cooperation.

In connection with the expansion of the guest group and of the potlatch protocol list, along with the increase in quantities of wealth goods involved, the expression of the precedence ratings—that is the actual order of distribution of gifts—clearly implies that earlier Southern Kwakiutl potlatches were small-scale affairs. The emphasis in the sequence of giving is not on tribal orders but on the namima sequences of rank within each tribe. If we disregard for a moment the matter of the eagles, considering only the real chiefs, the distribution invariably proceeded as follows: Gifts were given first to the chiefs of the highest ranked guest tribe, beginning with the first chief of the highest ranked namima of that tribe, then proceeding in order

---

[16] A great potlatch given by a mamaleleqala chief, noted by Codere (1950:64–66) citing Boas, lists thirteen guest tribes and represents one of the first, if not the very first, inclusions of the Kingcome Inlet and Knights' Inlet groups in the Kkagyuł festival group. Codere also notes (1950:64, n. 8) some difficulties and contradictions in the various precedence lists, which become easier to understand once we note that the lists come from a period in which the pan-Kwakiutl potlatch protocol was being developed. The date of the above-mentioned mamaleleqala potlatch can only be estimated (Codere suggests between 1875 and 1885). If we accept Mr. Nowell's assertion that his brother's potlatch had the longest guest list up to that time, the mamaleleqala affair must have followed it in time.

with the other chiefs of his namima. The second chief in rank of this tribe, that is, the first chief of the second ranking namima, was the next to receive his gift, and his namima brother chiefs were given gifts in sequence, before beginning with the third ranking chief and his namima, and so on through all the namima of the tribe. Then the highest ranking chief of the second tribe in precedence was given his gift (following the lowest ranked position in the first tribe), and the same order was followed, namima by namima, before beginning with the third tribe. (Being a late development, the eagles may well be interpreted as reflecting potlatch expansion and consolidation of the various groupings such as the Kwagyuł confederacy, for they received according to their special sequence prior to all the real chiefs and with no regard to their namima affiliations.) The sequence of distribution to the chiefs clearly suggests that the standard ancient form of potlatch was the a'wi'sila, the potlatch given by the chief of one namima to the other namima of his own tribe.

Both of the principal informants independently called attention to the fact that the potlatch gift order differed completely from that followed at feasts, which was more completely integrated with tribal and even confederacy organization. In a seal feast given to the Kwagyuł confederacy, for example, the first chief of the kwagyuł (gwetɛla) was served a seal breast. Then the first chief of the kwɛxa, the second tribe in rank, was served a seal breast, and a like portion was served to the first chief in rank of the walas kwagyuł. (The extinct q'omkutis were supposed to have preceded the walas kwagyuł.) Next, the second ranking chief of each tribe, in the same tribal sequence, was served a seal flipper, the third ranking chiefs, likewise in sequence, were each served a similar portion, followed by the fourth chiefs in rank. The remainder of the seals were distributed generally to the lower ranking chiefs. If the main dish of the feast consisted of some other food, the chiefs were called forth to be seated at the named decorated feast dishes in the same sequential order. If the guests were of a single tribe, as, for example, the nimqic or the mamaleleqala, the first chiefs of the namima were served in order, then the second chiefs, following the namima sequence, and so on. This same sequence was followed on certain other occasions, such as that of speech-making at the sale of a copper. Logically this feast sequence seems to conform better to the Southern Kwakiutl concept of relative rank in the expanded guest group than does the potlatch gift order. The inference is that the feast pattern was permitted more flexibility than that of the formal potlatch.

It is convenient at this point to note a drastic change in potlatch procedure that occurred in 1926 or 1927. It was noted by Codere, from mention by Mr. Nowell in his autobiographic account, as especially noteworthy. This modification consisted in the complete abandonment of distributing gifts according to the order of rank. Instead, the chief giving a potlatch at Alert Bay went from house to house in geographical order accompanied by his secretary, a literate young man with pen and notebook, sometimes a speaker, and two or three others, usually friends of high rank. In each dwelling the chief announced the motive of the potlatch and the amount of the gift to be given to the head of the house and to any other member of the household having a potlatch place, this being duly noted by his secretary. The gift, if of money, was then given to the recipient. If bulky articles were to be given, as in a flour feast, they were delivered by young relatives of the giver soon after. Theoretically it would have been possible, perhaps, to have made the rounds of the houses in the village observing the sequence of rank; but the simple, more rapid procedure of beginning at one end of the village and proceeding from house to house in geographic order was adopted.

As Codere surmises, this procedural modification was introduced to circumvent the anti-potlatch law. It appears that, in order to convict violators of the law arraigned before provincial courts, a rule-of-thumb definition of a "potlatch" had to be devised. This definition came to include "an assembly of Indians," an interpretation by the courts required for proof of an "Indian festival, dance or other ceremony," the language of the revised act. The Indians deliberately devised this "secret potlatch" procedure because they knew that not only were the proceedings less conspicuous and thus less likely to attract the agent's attention, but in addition they made it more difficult for him to prove a charge and get a conviction in the courts. The elimination of the public assembly feature of the potlatch seems to have been a sort of by-product, or accidental result, of early efforts to conceal the fact that a potlatch was being given, but it came to be regarded by the Indians as important when the chiefs met and decided to follow the new method at Alert Bay.

One element of the new potlatch form, however, the use of secretaries to record amounts of gifts and the like, was no novelty. The literate young man with pen or pencil and notebook had replaced the old-fashioned tallymen almost as rapidly as the Alert Bay Residential School produced graduates with reasonable competence in the three R's. This was not a Southern Kwakiutl specialization; all groups who continued their potlatching in any form put their newly gained literacy to this use.

Another subterfuge, which was like the preceding a major departure from former custom and practiced by persons resident at Alert Bay, consisted in carrying the potlatch to the guests rather than inviting the guests to the potlatch.[17] Sometimes potlatches or feasts were given piecemeal, so to speak. Mr. Whonnuck was one of the many to do this. On two occasions he gave a portion of his feast at Village Island to the mamaleleqala and others, and then gave a second segment, so to speak, in Kingcome Inlet.[18] The special device involved in such potlatches away from home was that the giver had to claim some right through kinship, no matter how remote, to be able to request the use of a house to give his potlatch in at a village not his own. Sometimes a very ancient intertribal marriage was the basis of the relationship invoked for this purpose. At Village Island Mr. Whonnuck could use the house of his wife's father's brother. At

---

[17] Cf. Halliday (1935) as cited by La Violette (1961:85-86).

[18] It must be noted that for many years most of the Kwagyuł, as well as the nimqic and various individuals of other groups, have resided at Alert Bay, originally because of the agent's orders and subsequently because of the commercial activity and consequent work opportunities there; Fort Rupert offered nothing but subsistence fishing and a little trapping.

Kingcome Inlet he used the house of a chief of a namima from which an ancestress of his wife's, three or four generations removed, had come.

Mr. Nowell had devised one of the most ingenious schemes to circumvent the anti-potlatch law. It was never actually carried out because the dropping of the article prohibiting the potlatch from the Indian Act made the maneuver pointless, but the idea is worth noting as typical of the Indians' ingenuity. There was a hospital at Alert Bay which was generally regarded as performing a very important service in the region. It received financial support from various sources, among them logging companies working in the area and the Indian Department, which gave a certain sum annually for services to Indian patients, and so on. Additional funds were often needed, however, and local residents periodically held fund-raising drives of one sort or another. In the late 1940's the Indian residents decided to contribute in their own way. They put on an annual show in the community hall, staging Kwakiutl dances and using such masks and other regalia that had escaped sale to museums or confiscation by the police. They charged admission to the performance, turning over the total proceeds to the hospital as the Indian contribution. Mr. Nowell's idea was this: there was a certain young man (a kinsman) who had a number of masks and other items of regalia that represented some important hereditary privileges. Mr. Nowell wanted to persuade him to display this paraphernalia with appropriate dances at the annual show, then to give a "private" (house-to-house) potlatch, formally stating his claims to the privileges publicly displayed. He would thus make the public display of his privileges, despite the law, and give his potlatch. The law against potlatching was removed from the books just in time to forestall this scheme.

Dan Cranmer's potlatch, given in 1921, was one of the largest in terms of wealth given away in Southern Kwakiutl history, and it was also the greatest legal debacle of the Kwakiutl. There was an Indian constable who participated actively in the preparations, assisting in dressing the dancers and so forth. He made copious notes after each part of the performance, which lasted several days, noting names and activities of all participants. These notes he turned over to the agent. Virtually all the Southern Kwakiutl were involved in one way or another. Twenty-nine persons who had played important parts were charged, tried, and convicted.[19] According to Mr. Nowell the list included the people of highest standing in the Kwakiutl system; he used to refer to the affair wryly as "that big potlatch, the one that got us all in trouble." Subsequently, a number of individuals who had been active in the potlatch up to that time ceased all participation in it.[20] Most of them did so properly and in good faith, but there were said to have been some individuals who took the opportunity to evade heavy financial obligations, in loans or completion of payments for coppers. In the 1930's the practice of making loans for potlatch purposes was formally stopped, and transactions in coppers had become few.

Regarding the coppers, the system broke down because of the introduction of the credit principal into the sales. Coppers had become rather scarce, even the patched-up and broken ones (which, Codere to the contrary, began their new cycle at a lower evaluation), and their prices were very high. From very ancient times a preliminary payment had been made to complete the agreement to purchase a copper, referred to by a term that meant the "pillow" (on which the copper would be placed); but a copper was not turned over to the buyer until full payment had been made. In late years, however, the pillow came to be accepted as a sort of down payment, comparable to that in white credit buying, so that the buyer took the copper, agreeing to complete the purchase at some future date. Since there was no way through processes of Canadian law to press a claim for a debt related to an illegal activity, various persons defaulted on their obligations. A number of instances were related in which coppers were resold, not once but several times, and finally

---

[19] Others who had participated in minor roles received the same treatment; all were equally guilty under the law. Halliday (1935:191 ff.) says that "eighty persons" were arrested on this occasion.

[20] This was initiated apparently by the court's action in offering suspended sentences to those who signed a formal agreement to do no more potlatching (cf. Halliday, 1935:190–192).

broken, with only the down payment's having been made. This is not meant to imply that defaulting on loans and indebtedness for copper purchases began in 1921; it had been happening occasionally for many years. As the informants pictured it, however, there were so many defaults following the 1921 trials that the chiefs eventually agreed to cease the practice of loans and credit sales of coppers, so that copper transactions nearly came to a standstill, although an occasional one has subsequently been made.

In addition to changes in the potlatch, over the years a number of changes were introduced into the Shamans' Society performances (Winter Dances) as well as the acquisition by a few chiefs of a second ceremonial, the dluwulaxa, from the Awikeno and Bella Bella. One of these was the publicly announced modification (to be described in more detail in another place) that dummies instead of actual human bodies would be used by the Hamatsa dancers in their cannibal feasts and that the biting of flesh from the arms of certain chiefs would be simulated. A second and in some respects even more significant change was the exclusive use of a much abbreviated version of the ceremonial. In former days a Shamans' Society performance was a very lengthy affair. For a number of decades only a condensed version in which the whole plot was represented in four or five days was staged. The most recent performance prior to the 1953 field trip was one given at Gilford Island in 1950. Mr. Nowell commented in passing that it had been so long since a complete performance had been given he was certain it could no longer be done properly—no one remembered all the details and exact sequences of the ancient version of the Shamans' Society rite. The obvious reason for this condensation of the ceremonial was that the prolonged absence of large groups of people attending the performance was certain to attract the attention of the agent and invite his unwelcome investigation. We do not know if the short form of the Shamans' Society rite was developed entirely in response to administrative pressure or if there was a special short version in aboriginal times as there was, for example, among the Nootkan groups in their variant of the Shamans' Society ritual. As will be noted, there was a one-night performance used by the Southern Kwakiutl in connection with mortuary rites, but this seems to have consisted of a series of selections of dances and was not a synthesis of the entire plot of the rite. In any case, the important fact is that the ceremonial was not discontinued, as Codere surmised (although the matter is not a crucial aspect of her argument), but that it, like the potlatch that was its invariable accompaniment, was adjusted by the Indians for survival in the climate of administrative hostility intended to abolish both institutions.

The foregoing describes some of the major changes in the potlatch during the historic period. Other changes, derived by inference rather than from the factual statements of informants, will be suggested. The two not altogether mutually congenial trends noted previously—the expansion of the institution correlated with the expanding wealth economy of the Southern Kwakiutl and its modifications to protect it from administrative sanctions—clearly represent the essential patterns of the changes. There is, however, a more subtle and stable pattern that must be noted; despite all the variety of outward changes of form connected both with the expansion of the institution and with its going underground, nowhere is there a suggestion of deviation from the original prime purpose of the potlatch—the formal presentation of a claim to hereditary right to a specific social status, or to hereditary privileges intimately related to such a specific status.

The Question of the Double Return of the Potlatch Gift

With these preliminaries out of the way, we turn to an aspect of the functional operation of the potlatch, or, to phrase the matter more candidly, we turn to early descriptions of the Southern Kwakiutl potlatch that make it very difficult to understand how the institution could possibly have functioned. We refer to the assertion made by Boas in his basic accounts that each potlatch gift put the recipient under obligation to return, when he in his turn gave a potlatch a year later, twice the number of blankets or other wealth items that he had received, and, moreover, that this double-return obligation continued indefinitely, resulting in an endless "pyramiding" or geometric progression of the obligations. In practical terms such a system is unworkable. The Kwakiutl of Boas' day were not potlatching one or two or three blankets at a time, they were giving them away by the hundreds and even thousands; and many chiefs were giving potlatches. A chief who attended, as he was obliged to do, a considerable number of these functions would incur a huge indebtedness if he had to repay all the gifts in amounts multiplied by two. Should he discharge such alleged obligations honorably, he would be entitled to some handsome returns; but if the twofold returns were made to him subsequently his indebtedness would be monumental. It is possible to devise fictitious examples of potlatch exchanges to dramatize the awesome totals that a literal application of this principle would add up to, beginning, for example, with a one-thousand blanket potlatch and carrying through half a dozen returns, or linking the some six hundred and fifty potlatch places in a sequence of gifts returns on such a basis. Such a presentation, however, does not really prove anything except the conceptual difficulty of the "double-return" interpretation.

It is worth noting that this is one of the points on which

Codere contradicts Boas. She specified that, although there did exist the concept of the twofold return (100 percent interest) in connection with loans (a fact noted also by Boas), the potlatch gifts were quite independent and apart from the loans and created no such obligation.[21]

Codere attempts to justify Boas' assertion regarding the double return by suggesting that although the quantities of blankets that would become involved in an endless pyramiding of this sort would soon become impossibly great, the system actually operated on the basis of fictitious credits—transfers of obligations to pay great quantities of nonexistent blankets. The inevitable collapse of such a system, she suggests, was prevented by the frequent writing off of the credits through the breaking of coppers. Her hypothesis is ingenious but untenable, as we shall demonstrate.

The question of the double return is more than just a casual detail related to the operation of the Southern Kwakiutl potlatch. It has affected the interpretation of the entire potlatch complex in two quite different ways. In accepting the view that it actually was part of Southern Kwakiutl practice, some writers, including Miss Codere, see in it additional evidence for their view that the potlatch of the Southern Kwakiutl was basically unique and different from that of other groups of the Northwest Coast. The other error to which the concept has contributed has been that of uncritical fieldworkers; they have tried to force their data from neighboring groups who did not practice the double return of potlatch gifts into the mold as described by Boas.[22] It is because of the broader theoretical implications that we consider clarification of the matter important.

---

[21] The confusion of loans and potlatch gifts is reflected in Boas' hypothetical example of the youth getting his financial start for potlatching, cited and carefully diagramed by Codere (1950:71–72). When the young man collects on his loans and pays his debts, he is ready to begin potlatching but has nothing to potlatch with, as Miss Codere's diagram proves. This demonstrates the physical law that a man cannot lift himself by his own bootstraps. Miss Codere has to spot him fifty blankets "from his father" to set him up in business; had he started with these fifty blankets in the first place, he would have saved much time.

[22] See Wike (1957:312–313) referring to Lopatin on Haisla.

Refutation of an assertion of this kind presents a certain methodological challenge. Our presentation will follow this order: (1) present informants' specific statements on the matter; (2) observed use of tangible wealth goods in Southern Kwakiutl potlatches; (3) special devices aimed at getting tangible wealth goods into potlatch transactions; and (4) data on certain instances in which credit systems broke down.

We have deliberately stressed the qualifications of the two principal informants, Nowell and Whonnuck, to bring out the fact that the two men were exceptional. Both were well versed in the potlatch, both were highly intelligent, and both could express themselves clearly. Therefore, their generalizations, as well as the specific instances they cited, must be given considerable weight. Both men flatly denied the endless chain, double-return principle. They made, independently, the same distinction that Curtis pointed out, that there was a type of loan—made ordinarily in blankets, later in money (although occasionally other items, such as cans of olachon grease, could be loaned on the same basis)—that required a double return, that is 100 percent interest, but that such loans were quite apart from potlatch gifts. A man with wealth to lend out might make public announcement of the fact, or he might let it become known through casual conversations. The borrower or borrowers came to him voluntarily, requesting loans in whatever amount they needed or wanted. The lender could in no case force the loan upon another person. The rate of interest was specified at the time of the borrowing. A loan requiring 100 percent interest was one made for a long term; if a loan was made for a short period at a lower rate, again the term and interest rate were agreed on when the loan was made. The gift made on the occasion of a potlatch had no such conditions, explicit or implied. From previous experience as an informant, Mr. Nowell suggested linguistics as a line of evidence, pointing out that the term for a loan (long term, at 100 percent interest), di'donum, had no distinguishable relationship to the term for potlatch gift, yaq!wima.

The value of potlatch gifts previously made by other chiefs to the giver of a potlatch did have a bearing on the amounts he gave those individuals; but both Mr. Nowell and Mr. Whonnuck were emphatic that such previous gifts were but one of the several factors involved in setting the amounts given. Relative rank of the recipients was another factor, although both informants brought out the point that the importance of relative rank of the guests, formerly the crucial factor in scaling amounts of gifts, had lessened in importance with the development of potlatching by all the chiefs, as we have indicated earlier. Another factor, and a more important one for practical purposes, was the total potlatch capital the giver planned to distribute. The amounts of both major and lesser gifts in a potlatch at which a thousand blankets were to be given away of course differed from the amounts of gifts at a five-thousand-blanket affair. The rule was that a guest who had previously given a substantial gift to the host, in a major potlatch, should be given a larger gift, but whether it should be *slightly* larger or *much* larger depended on the total amount the giver had available for distribution. In fact, if the potlatch given previously by the guest had been a very much larger affair than the current one and the gift to the current host thus had been much larger than he could be expected to give, etiquette could be salvaged by presentation of a gift notably larger than that to any other guest, even though it was less than the previous one. A mamaleleqala chief to whom Mr. Whonnuck had on one occasion given six cans of olachon grease at a grease feast subsequently gave a grease feast at which he gave the informant two cans of grease. The informant accepted with fairly good grace; his fellow guests received only a single can apiece, for it was a rather small-scale affair. The important thing was that his prior gift was recognized relatively if not in absolute amount. Only when a gift was both niggardly and failed to acknowledge a previous one did chiefs protest, demanding more from the host. Briefly, the informants left no doubt that they recognized no formal principle requiring the return of double the amount of a gift given in a potlatch.

A point made by both Mr. Nowell and Mr. Whonnuck was that the giver of a major potlatch took for granted that, although the gifts he made to some of his guests would eventually be reciprocated, many of the gifts would not, for the reason that some of his guests would not give another major potlatch, and others, when they did, might not include the giver's tribe and therewith the giver among their guests. As Boas himself noted, the major potlatch of any chief's career was usually given on receipt of the repayment of the bride price for his wife. In addition, a chief active in the potlatch normally gave a limited number of other potlatches that could be classed as major affairs. It was manifestly impossible for any chief to give as many potlatches as those he attended as a guest. Hence, the informants pointed out, it was accepted as inevitable that a sizable number of the gifts would never be reciprocated but were irrevocably "lost."

It might be asked if these assertions by the informants reflect change in potlatch custom in recent decades. We are certain that they do not. For one thing, in their descriptions of changes in formal procedure that have occurred in the potlatch during their lifetime and even before, both men displayed considerable historic sense. It seems possible that an interest in such matters was a pattern of Kwakiutl culture, related to the whole stress on inheritance of traditional rights and statuses. In addition, Mr. Nowell, pencil and notebook in hand, was taking active part in potlatch affairs as his elder brother's secretary when Boas began his intensive studies among the Southern Kwakiutl; thus, had the double-return pattern described by Boas actually prevailed at that time, he would have been cognizant of it.

The next aspect of our presentation emphasizes the Southern Kwakiutl interest in tangible rather than in fictitious credit; wealth articles in very large quantities were actually observed by Boas and others who witnessed Southern Kwakiutl potlatches. This point is noted by Codere, who calls attention to the photographs Boas published showing quantities of blankets displayed at such festivities. Such displays formed a prominent part of the predistribution demonstration, especially in the days when trade blankets by the bale were used in potlatches. Mr. Nowell, referring to his brother's greatest potlatch, noted that "the bales of blankets were stacked up nearly to the roof, clear across the back of the house" (that is, inside the house close to the rear wall). Sacks of flour for flour feasts were likewise piled up neatly and impressively in the days before the agents managed to force concealment of all these operations. It is apparent then that the Kwakiutl were interested in real tangible wealth items—blankets, money, flour, olachon grease, and the like—not imaginary riches.

As part of the proof of this principle we point to the various pump-priming devices for getting real blankets or hard cash into the operation. One aid was the concept, integrally related to the system of loans, that the lender had the right to demand repayment ("to call in his loans" as the informants usually phrased it) only when about to give a potlatch or to buy a copper—which was related, for proceeds of the sale were always immediately distributed in a potlatch—and thus needed both capital and interest for this purpose. Short-term loans were arranged when the lender had progressed in his planning to the point where he could specify just how soon he would be giving his potlatch, at which time he would demand repayment.

There were other devices having the same goal. Codere cites a portion of Mr. Nowell's biography, as given by Ford, concerning the purchase of a copper by Nowell's father-in-law as the main part of the bride-price repayment. Chief lagyus (Ford renders the name as "Lagius") is described as giving one thousand dollars as a down payment to finalize the agreement to purchase the copper from a ławitsis chief; this was the payment customarily referred to as the "pillow" for the copper: "Then he [lagyus] counted out the thousand dollars, which the tlowitsis chief took and said to all the people: 'This money is ready to be loaned out. At the time Lagius will pay for my copper, I will collect this money, which is to be paid 100 per cent back to me [i.e., paid back to the ławitsis chief plus 100 percent interest], and then it will be paid to Lagius.' "[23] This means that the so-called "pillow for the copper" payment was actually treated as a loan by the buyer of the copper to the seller. The seller (in the account cited, the ławitsis chief) manipulated it by relending it in smaller amounts during the period in which the buyer was assembling his resources to com-

---

[23] Codere (1950:73) citing Ford (1941:169–170).

plete the formalities of the purchase; then the seller returned the thousand dollars, plus the accrued interest, to the buyer who used both capital and interest in the final payment. The obvious point to this rather complex maneuver was to get real cash, not hypothetical credits, into the final sale, and subsequently into the potlatch to be given by the seller of the copper.

A similar sort of operation relating to the purchase of a copper and the subsequent potlatch by the seller was the giving of advances on the potlatch gifts (ts!owiltsum, an advance). Codere notes (1950:75) this procedure also, but the data available to her did not make its real significance clear. We shall cite a specific instance of such an operation later on. Here we use the designators B for the buyer of the copper and S for the seller. B has various sums loaned out at the standard long-term 100 percent interest rate, payment of which he is now entitled to demand in order to assemble his wealth for the purchase of the copper. Certain of his debtors find themselves short of cash, or blankets when blankets were in use. They are also, and this is an essential condition of this procedure, members of the groups being invited to the potlatch to be given by S with the proceeds of the sale. An agreement is made between B and S, and, as the Indians express it, S "assists" or "helps" B in assembling purchase money by giving the indigent debtors "advances" on their potlatch gifts, giving them, that is, the equivalent of the capital they had borrowed from B. The interest payment the debtors have to get elsewhere. The informants specified that, at least for small and even for moderate sums, no attempt was made to restrict the "advance" to the amount the debtor would ordinarily receive in the potlatch. If he owes twenty or twenty-five dollars to B, S "advanced" him that amount, even though the debtor normally would have been given only ten or fifteen dollars in cash as a potlatch gift. The debtors then liquidate their accounts with B. Both B and S keep careful account of the amounts involved. When actual purchase of the copper takes place, B turns over the total of the advances thus given out by S as a lump sum, plus the 100 percent interest payments. This sum is at once part of the purchase price of the copper and the repayment with 100 percent interest, of a loan by S to B.

When, in his potlatch, S comes to one of the persons to whom he gave such an advance, he (or his speaker) calls the person's name, then announces, "You have already received your gift." A token, such as a notched stick or other symbol, was usually given to symbolize the present.

Here again is a clear instance of the aim of the Indians to get real wealth, not credits, into the transaction. The seller of the copper went to great lengths to make sure he would be paid in real blankets or hard cash that he could physically distribute in his potlatch, not in "transfers of credit obligations." This point is highly important. The Southern Kwayiutl were familiar with a concept of simple credit, a loan of wealth goods, in later times Canadian currency, which had to be returned with interest after a shorter or longer period of time, depending on the agreement at the time of lending. There is no direct evidence at all to indicate that these credits were transferable. Even under what would seem to be the obvious circumstances of the model just described, *credits* were not transferred. B, the buyer, was assuming an obligation to pay S an amount of wealth goods for a copper. B did not say, "X owes me 25 blankets, plus 25 in interest, you, S, collect them from him and credit me with 50 blankets on the copper deal." B actually collected the 50 blankets from debtor X, then formally paid them to S, whether or not an "advance" from S was involved. (Halliday specifically describes this procedure in his synthetic potlatch story [1935:25–25].) Codere's easy-way-out hypothesis of credit transfer is not substantiated by the facts of Kwakiutl financial procedure.

It may be noted that the fact that the system of advances was a makeshift, not an ideal solution, was not lost on the people. Mr. Nowell remarked in discussing it that many chiefs deliberately tried to do as much lending as possible to members of their own tribe, since such debtors would not be in a guest status at the lender's potlatch and hence could not request advances of their potlatch gifts.

The final phase of our presentation of evidence against the endlessly pyramiding double return of the potlatch gift consists of instances in which extension of uncontrolled or uncontrollable credit caused the breakdown of the system. Several such instances, dating from recent times, will be cited. One derived from divergent value patterns imposed by acculturation; two instances might be characterized as short-lived inflationary excesses. One of the latter was in some respects similar to Codere's endless, or nearly so, "transfers of fictitious credits." The important fact, however, that the credits actually involved were uncontrolled or uncontrollable made the systems inoperable. Our thesis here is this: if these experiments in manipulating the credit concept, involving as they did something other than meticulous repayment of obligations in real material wealth goods, inevitably collapsed in a short time, then Codere's postulate of fictitious credits could not possibly have survived the many decades that she assumes it did. We insist that had imaginary, not real, wealth been the basis of potlatch finance, the entire potlatch system would have fallen apart long ago.

Mention has been made of the disruptive effects of the defaulting on debts, loans and the final payments on coppers, that occurred frequently after 1922. Solution was found and the potlatch survived when the chiefs formally abolished loans and credit sales of coppers. Defaulting for a time nearly acquired the status of a pattern, because as indicated native public opinion had lost its massive solidarity. The defaulter, usually announcing that he was abandoning the potlatch, not that he was defaulting on certain obligations, if he won the scorn of the conservative majority, also won the approbation of the agent, the missionary (especially the Pentecostal missionary when that sect was introduced), and the small but vocal circle of partisans of these two acculturational figures. Creditors had no effective redress, which is what was meant by the term "uncontrollable credit" previously used. Native sanctions formally brought to bear in connection with potlatching activities were not effective, because the defaulter, for the time at least, dissociated himself from the potlatch; the agent's authority and Canadian law could not be involved, for the plaintiff would incriminate himself of having engaged in illegal acts. With no way to enforce payment of obligations, uncontrollable credit in other words, the potlatch and traffic in coppers was almost disrupted. Only the action of the chiefs saved the situation.

Unregulated credit also appears to have been the principal factor causing the collapse of Lekwiltok potlatching. The Lekwiltok did not use coppers. Instead they used canoes in their potlatches and related transactions much, although not exactly, as other Southern Kwakiutl used the copper plaques. Some of these canoes were hulks of the ancient "war canoes," rotting serenely on the beach above tide line. Others seem to have been hypothetical canoes, or else were memories of ancient craft of which no physical traces remained. Our data are somewhat contradictory on this point, and in addition the Lekwiltok themselves seem to have become somewhat confused. It is clear, however, that as the huge canoes ceased to be made their value increased enormously, and the people developed an intricate system of holding shares in the old hulks and in the nonextant ones as well. The Lekwiltok bought and sold the canoes, and also parts of them, and gave them in marriages and potlatches. Some individuals appear to have resold shares that they had not completely paid for, as happened in the late copper dealings of other tribes. There came to be a state of complete confusion, apparently partly because of the unregulated credit and partly because of the breakdown in bookkeeping— the recording of the values of canoes and shares, payments made, and who owned what. It is said that Lekwiltok potlatches usually ended in squabbles and altercations over these matters.

In the early decades of this century the Lekwiltok occasionally began to attend potlatches of other Southern Kwakiutl. They learned about coppers but made no attempts to acquire them until Chief Billy Assu became the first of his tribe to own one since, if family traditions are to be believed, the original ancestor of the tribe lost a box of coppers at the Nimkish River. He bought a copper at Alert Bay with the express design of resolving the endless bickering and confusion in Lekwiltok potlatching by substituting coppers for canoes. But his people never took to the coppers. Finally the squabbles over canoe shares became so prevalent that Chief Assu, a dominant figure among his people, forced them to abandon the potlatch completely.

It is the case of the Kingcome Inlet "checks," on which we

have the most complete record, that we offer as proof of the proposition that a financial system of the sort envisaged by Codere, of credits based on nonexistent capital, could not continue to operate for long, let alone indefinitely. It was a system of fictitious credit which was attempted only to collapse in a relatively short time.

Mr. Whonnuck made the first reference to the incident when he was recounting his experiences during a trip to Kingcome Inlet to give an olachon grease feast. He was then given a return feast (the circumstances surrounding the initial feast and its return will be discussed separately since they were parts of an especially complex procedure). At any rate he was given a considerable quantity of olachon grease: "They gave me three or four thousand dollars worth of their damn no-good 'checks' too," he added with a grin. "They weren't any good, so I threw them away when I left the inlet." Query about the "checks" elicited a brief account of their origin and use, which was subsequently corroborated by Mr. Nowell. Later Mr. Nowell had the opportunity of discussing the topic with the man who had devised the potlatch check system, relaying this account to the field ethnographer. All three versions were essentially the same, indicating that the incident was well known; but the third, being somewhat more detailed, will be presented here.

The so-called checks were devised by a Kingcome Inlet chief whose English name was George Scow. On an occasion, apparently in the early 1920's, Scow was selling a copper named adimkwuli, valued at $15,000, to Chief qiqaqolas. His purpose, of course, was to potlatch with the proceeds of the sale. Qiqaqolas was selling a small copper of modest value to Chief wai'qas, also of Kingcome Inlet, to add to his funds for the big operation. Wai'qas had loaned small sums of money to various individuals, and since he was buying a copper he had a right to demand repayment. His debtors were all short of cash—perhaps qiqaqolas had gotten to them first. To resolve this problem, the debtors went to George Scow, requesting that he give them their potlatch gifts in advance. He gave to each one the amount of the original loan from wai'qas, recording names and amounts. It did not matter how much the debtor might have been given in the potlatch; if he had borrowed twenty dollars from wai'qas, Scow gave him that amount, even though in the potlatch distribution he would normally have been given only ten dollars. Each debtor then got the 100 percent interest from other sources, paying off Chief wai'qas. Wai'qas was then to pay the total of these advances plus interest to qiqaqolas, giving it as a separate sum since it was treated as a loan from Scow.

This particular instance was more than usually complex because of the intervention of the third party, wai'qas, but the giving of advances by the seller of a copper to debtors of the buyer was common practice among all Southern Kwakiutl, as previously mentioned.

On this particular occasion Scow had advanced a total of $400 to the debtors of wai'qas. The latter therefore should have repaid this sum in the amount of $800 in his purchase of the small copper, so that qiqaqolas might turn it over intact to Scow. Wai'qas, however, gave only $750 as repayment of the advances. Scow was furious; he took the view that the missing $50 was not from the interest payments but was a part of the cash he had laid out to expedite the sales. There was a bitter altercation, but wai'qas stolidly refused to pay the $50.

Sometime later Scow sold another important copper. Resolved not to let himself be shortchanged again, he introduced the check concept. He did it in this way: to the debtors of the buyer who requested their gifts in advance, he gave, instead of real cash, slips of paper on which he wrote the individual's name and the amount advanced, and affixed his signature. We were not able to collect samples of these documents, but they were described as following the form of the usual Canadian and U.S. bank check. By this date, the 1920's, the Kwakiutl were familiar with such instruments and used the English term "check" for them. The debtor then turned over his "check," along with the interest payment, to the buyer of the copper, the latter accepting the slips at face value in satisfaction of the debts in accord with his arrangement with Scow. In the actual procedure, the buyer gave the checks and the total interest payments to Scow in repayment of the latter's "assistance." When

Scow gave his potlatch he returned the slips to the recipients of the advances as receipts, along with the statement, "You have already received your gift."

This innovation rapidly developed certain flaws. We are not quite certain that "check" is the proper term for Scow's instruments, but if we retain the Kwakiutl usage, the paper slips that Scow distributed at his potlatch should have been designated "canceled checks." Many recipients did not understand this point, however, and began to circulate the pieces of paper as though they were still valid. The second defect was that other chiefs promptly began to emulate Scow. It was so easy to write a "check." Some of them, like Scow, were solvent financially and understood what they were doing, others were not and did not. Consequently within a short time fantastic amounts of worthless paper were circulating among the Kingcome Inlet groups in purchases of coppers, in potlatches, and in private transactions as well. Briefly, these tribes were doing something very similar to what Codere erroneously suggests all the Southern Kwakiutl were doing—potlatching with credits against a purely fictitious capital. There was even a concept of credit transfer involved in Scow's original idea, although it soon came to be warped out of all recognition.

At this time the Kingcome Inlet groups were potlatching principally among themselves in their winter retreat. It was only occasionally that other Kwakiutl managed to escape the agent's vigilance and join in the festivities. Those who did, however, soon realized the worthlessness of the checks, so that very soon no outsiders bothered to attend Kingcome Inlet potlatches. They accepted invitations only to grease feasts, for the grease was real and packed in real five-gallon tins (four imperial gallons); and if in addition they were presented with a few thousand dollars in checks, they wadded the pieces of paper up and threw them over the side, as Whonnuck did, on their way back down the inlet.

The real crisis, however, developed among the Kingcome Inlet people themselves. A few sagacious individuals loaned checks but demanded repayment in real money. There was almost no money in the potlatch. People who in the past had received good Canadian dollars hoarded them and potlatched with the checks, but there were those who protested. Squabbling and bickering over the checks became endless. Attendance at potlatches became sporadic and some chiefs threatened to abandon their places altogether. The Kingcome Inlet potlatch was on the verge of collapse when the chiefs, including George Scow himself, decided to stop the use of the worthless slips of paper and get back on the hard-money standard.

The foregoing instances are of interest for various reasons. They show that the Southern Kwakiutl were doing some experimenting with their wealth system: the delivery-on-downpayment procedure with coppers, the Lekwiltok share-system in canoes, the Kingcome Inlet checks. They also demonstrate very clearly that the native credit system was a very rudimentary one, rudimentary in the sense that it contained almost no regulatory mechanisms and safeguards, and thus did not admit elaborations. A defaulter, who in the accultural situation ceased participation in the potlatch, was impervious to the slights and gibes that were the only weapons of his creditors. The Indians understood and could operate with the simple loan, an arrangement between two persons in which a specified amount of wealth was loaned to be returned plus a specified amount of interest at a specified time (when the lender was going to give a potlatch). Even there credit problems arose: there were those who had to be dunned repeatedly and who, at the last moment, had to scurry about borrowing from Peter to pay Paul. It is clear from the instances cited that any attempt to elaborate on this simple-loan concept met with disaster. The basic cause of the inevitable failure of these innovations was the lack of adequate enforcing mechanisms. Thus, the Indians did not foresee the ramifications of their innovations, and hence did not plan against them. Such lapses in connection with innovation can occur in any culture. We of the world of modern technology did not foresee the socioeconomic effects of automation either.

Another point of interest here, although something of a side issue in relation to the principal discussion, is that the Southern Kwakiutl were not only willing to experiment with modifications of their potlatch and finance, but they were usually (except in the Lekwiltok instance) willing to discard innovations that did not work out. This flexibility, or ability to make realistic appraisals of cultural situations, was an important factor in enabling them to preserve their cherished institution despite many years of administrative pressure against it.

To resume our main argument, we believe that the foregoing data are of considerable weight in the refutation of Codere's construct that Kwakiutl potlatch finance was based on a system of transfers of credits against nonexistent capital. The native credit system—simple loans of real, tangible wealth items, repaid in items of identical reality—functioned successfully for many decades. On the occasions recorded when attempts were made to substitute intangibles or add them to the credit concept —the "shares" of the Lekwiltok canoes, the credit transfers involved in George Scow's checks—the system collapsed. This is why we are convinced that the case of the Kingcome Inlet checks is especially pertinent: it came to be in essence so like the system Codere asserts was standard practice in all Southern Kwakiutl potlatching. Note here that we are drawing a distinction between a unique experiment made by the Kingcome Inlet groups, which failed dismally, and the hypothetical traffic in fictitious values that Codere supposes operated successfully among all Southern Kwakiutl for many years. One can go further and say that had Codere's construct in fact prevailed, that is, continued successfully over the decades, the Kingcome Inlet people would not have had the trouble they did; the device of the checks would have been not a drastic change but simply a minor improvement, a little better than Codere's "tally-sticks."[24]

To sum up, the ideas of the continually augmenting "double

---

[24] Codere asserts that tally sticks served to represent the nonexistent valuables. This is not correct. Tally sticks were used, but to keep accounts of actual wealth items physically transferred by, for example, the buyer of a copper to the seller. Once the physical count had been made, it was manifestly easier to check totals by counting notches on tally sticks than by rehandling the thousands of blankets. Sticks were also used to symbolize canoes to avoid carrying the vessels from the beach and back again; but except among the Lekwiltok, real canoes of good, sound red cedar, not imaginary ones, were transferred.

return" obligation of the potlatch gift, first presented by Boas, then rationalized by Coderes' ingenious but fallacious hypothesis, is contradicted by a formidable array of factual evidence:

1. Flat denials by our informants, both of whom were authorities on potlatch matters, that the ordinary potlatch gift produced such obligation. In this they corroborated Curtis' data, recorded nearly forty years earlier.[25]

2. The actual distribution, observed by Boas and others, of huge quantities of blankets and other wealth items in potlatches.

3. The use of what we have called pump-priming devices, whose sole purpose was to get real wealth, not mythical credits, into the potlatch transactions.

4. Instances in which attempts were made to use intangibles or fictitious credits in the potlatch that rapidly proved inoperable.

In this connection it becomes necessary to comment on Codere's final step in her attempted solution to the mystery of the missing wealth. She proposes that the slate was cleared of all the cumulative obligations of nonexistent valuables when these were used to purchase a copper, which, when broken, wiped out all the debts. It is, in a sense, a pity that the Kwakiutl did not achieve this concept; they would have done some interesting things with it, or at least would have had some interesting experiences trying to make it work. The actual fact is that when a copper was broken or "drowned" no credits of any sort were wiped out. This was true even when simple credit had been involved in the purchase of the particular copper, in cases, for example, in which the full payments on the copper had not been completed. As reported earlier, several cases were related by the informants in which, during the brief vogue of the delivery-on-down-payment procedure in copper sales, the objects were broken by the presumptive purchaser, who then defaulted on the balance due. Thirty and more years later the sellers still maintained the unpaid amounts were owing to them. Chief Billy

---

[25] Incidently, George Hunt, Boas' interpreter-informant, seems to have been one of the principle contributors of ethnographic data in Curtis' work.

Assu of the Lekwiltok, for example, never completed payment on the copper he bought years ago to introduce use of coppers to his tribe; the amount he owed was common knowledge—and the seller's heirs were still resentful.

The topic of the double return cannot be dropped at this point, however, if we are to do it justice. It is here Drucker considers that his earlier flat statements might be regarded as oversimplification. His justification is that they were made in general discussions of cultural patterns of the entire area, where it was not appropriate to bring in such minutiae as may be presented in a specialized account like the present one. When Boas began collecting his data and subsequently, there actually were circumstances in which double the amount of the original quantity of blankets or money had to be returned. These situations did not involve potlatch gifts directly (aside from one complicating factor), and all of them without any exceptions were limited to a *single* repayment; that is, on repayment of double the amount originally given, all obligations by both parties ceased. Thus the principle that creates the logical difficulty—that of endless pyramiding—disappears.

There were two situations involving the double return, repayment of loans at interest and payment of the bride price in marriage. Successive sales of coppers involved something approaching the pyramiding principle, but buying was voluntary; no one was obligated to buy a particular copper. A new buyer appeared each time, and each sale ended obligations between that particular buyer and seller.

The loans were first described by Boas; there is little that can or need be added to his account. Long-term loans were made at a flat rate of interest of 100 percent, loans for half a year or so at 50 percent, and short-period loans returned 25 percent. There were minor exceptions; in the sale of a copper, as we mentioned earlier, the advances made by the seller to the debtors of the buyer (in English termed "help" or "assistance" to the buyer) were regarded as a loan by seller to buyer to be repaid at 100 percent, even though the blankets or money might be out of the "lender's" hands only a few days. However, in this instance the

100 percent interest actually came from the debtors of the buyer, who had held the loans for long periods of time. In any loan, as soon as repayment complete with interest had been made, all obligations of the debtor to the creditor ceased.

Loans were entirely distinct from the potlatch, except in one very specific way already noted; the lender could demand repayment only when he was about to give a potlatch or purchase a copper (which was regarded as a transaction connected with potlatching).

In Southern Kwakiutl culture the institution of marriage had certain very special features. First, the formal union of a couple of high rank was regarded as creating a bond not only between the man and woman concerned but also between their social groups, their namima that is to say, and by extension between their tribes and even the confederacies. (It must be understood that throughout this discussion primary reference is to those of high social status.) The fluidity of definition of "in-groups" and "out-groups," modified according to needs or interests of the moment, is identical to Nootkan usage in this regard (Drucker, 1951 *passim*). Another feature of marriage is that it was intimately connected with potlatching.

Boas reported the formal aspects of marriage among the Kwakiutl, emphasizing that they revolved about the payment of the bride price by the groom and/or his kin group, and later the payment of this bride price by the bride's group in about double the amount of the original payment. The repayment included names, masks, dances, and other privileges in addition to wealth goods, a concept that was clearly an expression of the bilateral basis of Kwakiutl society. We may note in passing that this inclusion of privileges in the bride-price repayment was not restricted to the Southern Kwakiutl, but was customary among all Wakashan-speaking peoples: Heiltsuk (except the definitely matrilineal Haisla) and Nootkans. In addition it was found among the Salishan Bella Coola, who were in many respects very similar culturally to their Heiltsuk neighbors, and among many nearby Coast Salish groups of the Georgia Straits region as well (Barnett, 1955:188 ff.). Many Heiltsuk names and privileges, such as the dluwulaxa Dancing Society complex, were acquired by Southern Kwakiutl through marriage of their chiefs to Awikeno and Bella Bella women of high rank.

The principal additions that may be offered to supplement Boas' account are explanatory details. Boas noted that the groom was under obligation to give a major potlatch as soon as he received the return of the bride price. We point out that there was great variation in the time interval between marriage and the repayment. A recipient might have been planning to stage an affair involving greater quantities of wealth than he could reasonably expect in the repayment, and under such circumstances he might not pressure his father-in-law to make the repayment promptly. Sometimes years intervened between payment of the bride price and the repayment. The great potlatch of Mr. Whonnuck's father's father is purported to have been financed by the marriage repayment, although the giver had accumulated additional wealth in considerable quantity. When the bride-price repayment was finally made, the product of the union (the informant's father) was a young married man who danced as Hamatsa in the Shamans' Society performance associated with the potlatch. In contrast, Mr. Nowell's father-in-law formally presented him with the repayment within a short time after the informant's marriage.

The amount of the repayment was at times not precisely fixed, although in principle it was supposed to be about two times the amount of the bride price in wealth goods. (Privileges were supplementary to what we may term the cash transfer; they were not rated in terms of blankets or dollars.) There appears to have been a tendency in more recent times, when money was used in both bride price and repayment, for the return to be computed more closely than in ancient days—the arithmetical result of the bride price times two. But sometimes more than two times or even three times the original amount was returned.

In unions regarded as of great social importance because of the rank of the couple concerned, nothing less than a copper was felt to be adequate as repayment. The copper had to be sold so that a potlatch could be given. Mr. Whonnuck's father received two coppers in the marriage repayment, one from his wife's nimqic mother's brother and the other, a copper that had cost four thousand blankets, from Mr. Nowell's elder brother, then chief of the kwɛxa and a close paternal kinsman of the woman. (It goes without saying that both these chiefs had received large bride-price payments.) This pattern was susceptible to various practical modifications. For example, if the father-in-law was not sufficiently solvent or for some other reason did not want to become involved in the purchase of an expensive copper, and the son-in-law insisted on being given such a one, the son-in-law himself would contribute the large sum necessary to provide the difference between the repayment and the price of the copper. Mr. Nowell's elder brother assisted Chief Iagyus in the purchase of the copper given to Mr. Nowell. A mamaleleqala chief, whose English name was Amos Dawson, purchased a copper in the amount of 23,000 blankets ($11,500) from Mr. Nowell's elder brother for this purpose. This payment did not consist entirely of blankets but included some cash money, several canoes, and two small, inexpensive coppers. Dawson's father-in-law contributed a relatively small amount, although he was the nominal purchaser. The major portion of wealth was provided by Dawson himself. The informants did not spell it out, but obviously such arrangements were made at the time of setting the bride price and had a regulatory effect on the quantity concerned in that transfer.

To the Indians the significance of the large repayment and the potlatch given therewith was not simply as a means of manipulating and distributing wealth goods. To them the important consideration was that, in the potlatch given by the bride's group, the wealth goods were announced and displayed, and thus the right of the groom and of the couple's descendants to claim and use these items was publicly defined.[26]

[26] The distinction noted by Piddocke (1965:252) between "names and positions which could go out of the numaym [namima] [by gift to a son-in-law] and those which could not," which in effect would have created two simultaneous lines of inheritance, one patrilineal and one matrilineal, may have been a part of native theory, but was not strictly observed, at

The "mock marriages," described by Boas, to a chief's arm or foot or housepost or the like were referred to by our informants, who specified that, just as Boas related, the purpose of such extravagances was to acquire privileges. They mentioned a similar device, not regarded as a marriage but similar to the mock marriages, q!aqakwȧ ("buying as a slave"), in which a chief's son was nominally purchased, to be redeemed in at least three times the original amount of wealth goods plus various privileges. The ideas of the mock marriages seemed faintly humorous to informants, as it is to us. The topic of motivation was not explored, but the few chiefs mentioned as having entered into such arrangements were all referred to as elderly. Perhaps they were of an age at which they did not wish to cope with a young bride.

Another elaboration of the bride price and its repayment was that the procedure could be gone through more than once. The first repayment was called oxLa'akw; a second repayment (called forth by a second payment of the bride price) was sȧp^{h}it. When Mr. Whonnuck went to Kingcome Inlet to give a grease feast, he did so as a repetition of payment of the bride price for his wife (who was not, properly speaking, from Kingcome Inlet but was related to a certain namima there). That was why he was given the return feast. At Kingcome Inlet he gave away fifty cans of grease, in addition to ten actually consumed. The repayment (sȧp^{h}it) by the Kingcome Inlet chiefs consisted of one hundred cans and the so-called checks. On this occasion Mr. Whonnuck publicly assumed a name,

---

least during the long years of population decline. The adjustment made was this: if there were no surviving sons or younger brothers to inherit an important name and position, these rights could be given to the son-in-law in trust for his son. While using these rights the son-in-law and later the grandson would be considered members of the donor's namima. Mr. Whonnuck, for example, used his nimqic title and other prerogatives only when he attended a feast or potlatch with the nimqic, when he was seated with the nimqic chiefs, and was treated as a member of that tribe and of the namima of his mother's mother's brother, from whom he had inherited the rights. In this sense it is true that certain important names did not go out of the namima; but the fluidity of group membership permitted such transfers out of the male line where necessary due to lack of direct male heirs.

kwɔxilanoqwɔmi, which had been given to him by his "father-in-law," actually his wife's uncle, with the first repayment.[27]

We have shown that the repayment of the bride price related the institution of marriage to the potlatch system and was for the specific purpose of transferring names and other privileges from the woman's group to her husband.[28] It is interesting to consider the legal effect of the repayment. The Southern Kwakiutl, like the Nootkans, regarded the repayment as theoretically canceling the obligation on the part of the woman to stay with her husband. When Chief Iagyus, Mr. Nowell's father-in-law, gave the copper, money, and various articles including dishes and furniture as repayment of the bride price, he said in the course of the speech he made, "y qowilàs is free now. She is ready to leave her husband. If there is any chief who wishes to marry her, let him ready his property to pay the bride price." However, y qowilàs continued with her husband all the many remaining years of her life. The same was true, the informant added, of many couples who married according to Indian custom. In a sense the wife's stay was thus voluntary.

The function of marriage as establishing formal relationship between the groups of the two partners had expression in various ways. The terms of marriage and bride price conveyed this concept. Marriage was called kadziL!a, explained as "meaning [not literally but by connotation] you walk [rightfully] into your wife's house," or, "you walk as an owner into your wife's house." Bride price, kadziLlm, was "that which permits you to walk into your wife's house." (There is another term for bride price, ts'yi.) The house referred to was, of course, the old fashioned structure that housed the entire namima. By extension, not only

---

[27] The fact that he did not formally assume this name during his first potlatch (on receipt of the first repayment) means that he was reserving it, apparently already planning on the second round of payments (he received no privileges with the second repayment).

[28] There was a difference in this regard between Kwakiutl and Nootkan usage. Among the latter, such transfers were specifically for the offspring of the union and their descendants; lacking offspring, the transfer was invalid. Southern Kwakiutl, however, irrevocably transferred privileges with the repayment.

the husband but all his namima were placed in the position of privileged relatives as a result of the marriage.

The Southern Kwakiutl, just like the Nootkans, met only their relatives in peace and friendship for feasts and festivals. Non-relatives were automatically enemies. The grouping of tribes described as the ancient potlatching groups were also the intermarrying groups, very closely linked by affinal ties renewed generation after generation—a relationship that was highly important to the Indians. Even in recent times the relationship principle was invoked in times of strain. About 1910 or 1912, Mr. Whonnuck's father invited many of the tribes to Fort Rupert. For one reason or another, the potlatch was not finished when the time came for people to go up Knight's Inlet for the olachon fishing. It was resolved that the guests would return to Fort Rupert the following winter until the potlatch was concluded. However, the chiefs of the ɬawitsis tribe invited certain of the guests to a potlatch, or perhaps had already invited them. Mr. Whonnuck went to see them. He was invited into the chief's house. The ɬawitsis men sat and lay about in sullen silence, refusing to look at him. "I tried to joke with them a little. Then I told them that they were [affinal] relatives of my father. Relatives should try to help each other. Our potlatch could not go on without them, and the other tribes were waiting at Fort Rupert; they could give their potlatch later. So finally they said they would come to Fort Rupert." The informant emphasized that his most effective argument was based on the point of kinship, although the actual kinship in this case was a remote one.

It was by the same sort of extension of the kinship principle that the financial transactions connected with marriage were telescoped with the potlatch. In connection with marriage, in addition to the bride price that a man gave to his future father-in-law, he might give a potlatch to the entire tribe to which his bride's namima belonged or to the other tribe or tribes to which she was related, designating such an affair as "a payment of bride price." This is what Whonnuck was doing when he gave the grease feast at Kingcome Inlet. His wife was related to a certain family line there, but for the purposes of the feast he treated the entire confederacy as her kin—as his fathers-in-law and brothers-in-law. Therefore, when he distributed fifty cans of grease among the chiefs (apart from the ten actually consumed at the feast) he obligated the recipients to return to him two cans for each one received.[29] This was the only situation in which a transfer of wealth goods, nominally made as a potlatch gift, created a fixed obligation for a double return. Repayment of the bride-price gifts ended the transaction. There was no continuing obligation. And it must be noted that this combination of potlatch and bride-price payment was not a common practice, nor did many chiefs pay the bride price a second time.[30]

There are many data available on the famous coppers.[31] In the transactions in which ownership of one of these objects was transferred, it was customary for each successive sale to be in a larger amount so that eventually many coppers came to have enormous values. In generalizing, informants commonly say that the value of a given copper doubled in each successive sale, but this was not invariably true. In the early sales, when the value of a specimen was still comparatively low, the price might be doubled or nearly doubled on each exchange. As the value reckoned on the basis of the last sale increased, the relative amounts of successive increases often tended to become more moderate. For example, the copper purchased by Amos Dawson for 23,000 blankets on a previously cited occasion had originally

[29] The Kingcome Inlet episode was actually only a part of the real grease feast given by the informant, for he gave grease also as a second payment of bride price to the Kwagyuɬ, mamaleleqala, nimqic, ɬawitsis, and tenaxtɔx, utilizing a total of 380 cans, including the 60 taken to Kingcome Inlet. The informant considered the distribution of the 380 cans to be a single affair. It was done piecemeal because of administrative pressure against potlatching. Mr. Whonnuck had made a potlatch occasion of his first bride-price payment also, inviting the same tribes.

[30] We interpret the incident cited by Dawson (1887:80) concerning the prospective giver of a potlatch who went from Alert Bay to Fort Rupert to invite the Kwagyuɬ, and at the same time "loaned" his future guests 500 blankets, which they returned in double amount, as being the same procedure as that carried out by Mr. Whonnuck.

[31] Codere is definitely in error on one point of her discussion of coppers: that "buying and selling . . . of a copper was done only between rivals." "Rivals" competed in *destroying* coppers, but sales transactions required a certain friendly attitude and cooperation, not enmity.

cost 400 blankets when it was first acquired by a Southern Kwakiutl from the "Sebassas." The complete history of this piece among the Kwakiutl was not collected, but Mr. Nowell stated that the copper had been purchased by his elder brother (who sold it to Dawson) for 20,000 blankets, and that Dawson eventually sold it to a nimqic chief for the same amount for which he had purchased it, namely 23,000 blankets. Mr. Nowell, at various times in discussions of coppers, stressed two points. One was that the selling price of expensive coppers did not automatically increase by any predetermined amount over the amount of the previous sale; depending on circumstances, the value of such a copper might go up two, three, or four thousand blankets at a time. The crucial factor, and this was Mr. Nowell's second point, was that the price exacted for a copper depended on the amount that the seller needed for the potlatch he was giving. Ordinarily the formal sale of a copper was a sort of curtain-raiser to a potlatch; that is to say, the potlatch guests were not only invited but actually assembled, so that the potlatch proper would begin as soon as the payments for the copper had been counted out and turned over. The seller thus had a specific amount that he had to assemble, depending on how many groups he had invited, and how much he intended to give to the various guests. Apparently there was some rather close figuring done during the informants' lifetimes, for both Nowell and Whonnuck often referred to chief's consultations with their secretaries during the proceedings to check the amount needed. This may seem a minor point, but it is not; for many published accounts of sales of coppers seem to stress the buyer and his payment rather than the seller and his requirements. Mr. Nowell noted that at times valuable coppers were sold at bargain prices, that is, for less than at their prior sales. Such a sale might be made in an emergency situation—for example, to give a mortuary potlatch in the event of a sudden death in a chief's immediate family. The chief would announce that he intended selling the copper so-and-so, which had cost such-and-such an amount, for whatever he might be offered in an immediate sale. A prospective buyer would offer as much as he could muster for immediate payment and the sale would be closed with no more ado. No discredit attached to either party in such an operation, for the emergency nature of the transaction was recognized by all the Indians. The seller had to accept what he might be offered to be able to potlatch on short notice; the buyer similarly had to assemble a large quantity of blankets or cash on the spur of the moment. This kind of transaction, although not normal procedure in selling coppers, was well enough recognized to have a name: dagyi:wi, "hold [the copper] with its head down."

The breaking of coppers in connection with rivalries has been reported in great detail by previous writers. However, it has not been emphasized that there were also usages somewhat closer to those of the northerners from whom the objects came. The pieces of a copper broken in connection with a mortuary potlatch were referred to as representing "the bones of the deceased," paralleling Tsimshian metaphor; and as among the same northern people, distribution of such pieces did not always entail a challenge to a rival. Mr. Nowell said it was his understanding that this method of use (that is, the breaking as part of the mortuary rites) was the more common one in ancient times.

Unbiased consideration of the whole pattern of institutionalization of the simple double return (a single return, not entailing an infinite succession of exchanges), as in loans at interest, marriage repayments, and to a certain point the resale evaluations of coppers, brings up the problem of its historic depth. There is no way to document the matter, but logic suggests that a concept probably represents an invocation made during the historic period under the stimulus of alien influences.

The system of loans, for example, with rate differentials according to time periods, inevitably strikes one as incongruous in native American culture patterns. The idea on the face of it seems more like one that might have been introduced by a Scottish factor doing a little under-the-counter loan-sharking at the fort. We have already pointed out that time was of little moment to the Kwakiutl even in such important matters as the marriage repayment. As long as the formalities were complied with, it mattered little whether the repayment was made in one year or twenty.

Using a similar approach, it may be seen that any concept involving doubling of returns with anything approximating exactitude necessarily depends on a scale of standardized values —units of value by which articles regarded in the culture as desirable could be calibrated—in short, a currency. The Hudson's Bay Company trade blankets provided such a device and, later, Canadian dollars fulfilled the same function, making it possible for the Indians to rate a canoe or a copper or a slave or a quantity of olachon grease in precisely comparable terms. There is absolutely no evidence that the Indians had any such exact measure aboriginally. No two sea-otter pelts were identical; one would be larger, another better furred, a third less damaged by the harpooning that brought it to boat. No two canoes, even of nearly the same size, would be admitted by experts to be exactly alike; one might be more stable but less maneuverable, and so on. There was no standard Southern Kwakiutl gallon for measuring olachon grease. As a consequence it becomes very difficult to perceive any way in which a quantity arithmetically twice that of another could have been precisely reckoned.[32]

What does seem to have existed in former times, both on grounds of simple logic and because it was a concept prevalent among neighbors of the Southern Kwakiutl, was the idea of making return gifts in certain situations that were manifestly larger, or more, than the original wealth transfer, with no attempt to define the return as 125, 150, 200, or 300 percent or any other exact quantity. The Nootkan groups, for example, in repaying the goods given as a bride price, simply gave great quantities of valuables in addition to the privileges, without attempting any exact measure. Among Tlingit and Tsimshian of

---

[32] Drucker (1965:50–51) has discussed the nonmonetary nature of aboriginal wealth on the north Pacific coast. In a certain sense even the famous blankets were not a completely stable currency, a point that causes confusion to all ethnographers but not to the Indians. The blankets once were priced by Hudson's Bay Company at $.50 each, or $1.00 per pair. This price changed by increase over the years. Hunt refers to the value of a bale of 50 blankets, presumably double ones, as being worth $125.00 (Codere, 1961:459), that is $2.50 per pair, or $1.25 each. In conversation, however, informants almost invariably convert blankets to cash in terms of the old $1.00 per pair evaluation.

recent times, a chief giving a potlatch might receive loans from his wife's brothers. Whether or not such lending was customary aboriginally, the return which was considered proper depended on a simple principle: The recipient of the loan eventually paid back the amount of the principle plus "a little more." There was no fixed rate for the "little more," nor prior arrangement between the parties concerned. The borrower added whatever he could. In some Tsimshian and Niska potlatch records shown to Drucker, he noted loans of $100 repaid with the addition of anything from $10 to $40. In fine, the idea of "a little more," vague and indefinite in measure, may have been an ancient element of the wealth goods manipulation among the Southern Kwakiutl, as well as among their neighbors, in connection with returns in certain situations; but the concept of the precise doubling of the original amount probably came in with the introduction of standard value units, the trade blankets.

Potlatch Controls and Other Mechanisms

An aspect of the Southern Kwakiutl potlatch that has not been sufficiently stressed in previous accounts, although some of the basic data were recorded, is that the potlatch was definitely not an institution that went freewheeling along, governed only by mysterious economic laws. This statement is not intended to suggest that economic laws did not apply; in fact we have here invoked something akin to an economic principle in regard to the inevitable collapse of a fictitious credit system. However, in addition to such principles as may have affected the potlatch, on the operational level it was very formally and rigidly controlled. The regulatory mechanism was the Council of Chiefs.

Boas' accounts make frequent mention of "a secret meeting of the chiefs," usually in connection with the planning for the Winter Dances or, as we refer to them, the Shamans' Society performances. This gives the essential clue as to the probable origin of the device. The Shamans' Society rites were very complex affairs, the more so when they were staged on a scale that involved the several namima of a tribe or all the tribes of the Kwagyuł. The same, as will be brought out, was true of the potlatch, even when given without the ceremonial. In the Shamans' Society performance, the chief who wished to sponsor the rite had to consider that other chiefs of his tribe might have Hamatsa initiates who had already begun to "go through" the ritual, and who necessarily had to participate. There were also many privileges in the various family lines—like Mr. Whonnuck's right to a certain type of grizzly bear performance—which the owners might wish to display. As a matter of fact there was in each tribe a tremendously long list of such special rights, major and minor. All these special acts were not staged in any single performance with the exception of the Hamatsa, since all active Hamatsa had to perform in certain phases of the ritual. Many, however, would be included. For each performer regalia had to be refurbished or made anew, novices had to be taught their routines, songs taught the singers; in short a great deal of preparation was necessary.

The fact that these ceremonials were primarily theatrical productions for the purpose of displaying hereditary privileges rather than predominantly religious rites has been brought out elsewhere (Drucker, 1955, 1965). The relevance of this point here is that, like any big show, a Dancing Society performance could not be put together in a day; and with use of privileges managed by various chiefs for their several namima a great deal of planning and coordination was necessary. Thus the chiefs met privately, "in secret" as Boas wrote, to plan the innumerable details. A potlatch, even when given without one of these theatrical displays, required similar coordination, especially when it was to be a major affair. According to the rating of the golden age, even a minor potlatch given by a chief as head of his namima to the namima of his tribe—"a potlatch to one's own tribe" as informants called it—required at least enough prior arrangement with the chiefs of the other namima to avoid conflicts in timing with some other festival planned by one of the intended guests. Potlatches on a larger scale in which a chief planned to invite another tribe or tribes from his position as a tribal chief required the cooperation of all his tribesmen and consequently necessitated advance planning by the chiefs. The giver's fellow chiefs would be called upon to make speeches; some might wish to give subsidiary feasts prior to the main event. The lower rank personnel of all the namima would be expected to assist in various ways, as singers, attendants, and general utility workers—carrying the bales of blankets and other articles to be distributed, and the like. The intent of this discussion is to emphasize that the potlatches as well as the more elaborate Dancing Society affairs often associated with them involved a great deal of preparation and planning, not only by the giver but by his fellow chiefs, which for practical purposes were dealt with by the chiefs in private conclaves.

The council of chiefs, a designation used most frequently by Mr. Nowell (Mr. Whonnuck usually said simply that "the chiefs met"), comprised all those of the tribe or, in the case of the

Kwagyuł, the confederacy who held places in the potlatch. Procedures of the meetings were informal by our standards; a problem was discussed at length until the pattern of the concensus of opinion became clear and assent of the group was given to whatever the generally approved proposal might be. There was no imitation of our parliamentary procedure; no one presided over the meetings; there was no formal voting. There was, therefore, no indication at all of alien influence or inspiration in the operation of the council of chiefs until, in the closing years of the past century, it became common at Fort Rupert at least for the chiefs to bring an educated young Indian to their meeting as a scribe to take any notes they might want recorded. Mr. Nowell often filled this role in his younger days. The *modus vivendi* of the meetings may strike us as clumsy and inefficient, but apparently the experience gained in coordinating ceremonial procedures and the like made it possible for the chiefs to make effective decisions.

Almost the sole theme of the discussions of the chiefs was the potlatch and the Shamans' Society rites often associated with it. Anything that was related to the potlatch in the broadest interpretation of the term was admissible to the agenda. The council of chiefs rarely took note of what we might call political or civic problems unless those matters impinged directly on the potlatch, so that as a consequence the council never became, properly speaking, a factor in Kwakiutl political organization.[33]

Mr. Nowell related an incident that took place in the 1890's of which he had special knowledge since he participated in certain portions of it. At the time of this incident the Indian agent was rather lenient in regard to the anti-potlatching law. That is, while he permitted none of the affairs to be given at Alert Bay and obliged the kwagyuł and a few other tribes to reside at that village, he often gave permission for the outsiders to return for a few weeks at a time to their home territories when they pleaded the necessity for laying in supplies of food,

---

[33] Mr. Nowell related an incident to Ford (1941:99) in which the chiefs met to deal with the problem posed by a man they believed to be an especially malicious sorcerer. However, their consideration of such a matter seems to have been highly exceptional.

and did not pry into their activities on these trips away from Alert Bay. Of course, every such vacation from the agent's authority was used by the Indians for potlatching.

On this particular occasion the Kwagyuł tribes were assembled at Fort Rupert. The elder, serious members of the community were dedicating their time to the potlatch. The restless younger set, however, were devoting their time to frivolity, principally philandering and heavy drinking. Among this disorderly group was a "young chief," that is a chief's son, who was enamored of the daughter of a commoner. He wanted to marry her, but when he formally requested her in marriage her father flatly refused. The refusal derived from the fact that the young chief, as part of the arrangement, intended to have a name of chiefly rank bestowed on his prospective father-in-law to cover up the lowly origin of his intended bride. Such a procedure would have been impossible aboriginally, but by this time there were lower ranking titles to all intents vacant that could be manipulated by the chiefs. The reaction of the girl's father to this was a decisive negative; he wanted no part of such a scheme. He was an old man, he said in effect, and he had been a commoner all his life. He knew nothing about the duties of a chief, he did not know the intricacies of the potlatch which was the business of the chiefs, and he did not feel that he would be able to handle these responsibilities. Therefore he would not let his daughter marry a chief.[34] Not long afterward the lifeless body of the young chief was found hanging from a tree behind the village. The fact that the corpse's feet were dragging on the ground aroused the suspicion that a murder, clumsily dis-

---

[34] It is an interesting commentary on real Southern Kwakiutl attitudes that the old man's logic seems to have been generally accepted as reasonable and proper by his contemporaries. This would scarcely have been the case had the "megalomaniac" or "self-aggrandizement" pattern that Benedict proposed actually dominated the culture. By such a standard, the old man should have been derided as abnormal and a fool rather than as native public opinion appraised him: as a sensible realist. The basis of the public opinion in this case lies in the Southern Kwakiutl appraisal of a chief's duties, particularly those relating to the potlatch, as heavy burdens that could be performed only by those trained from childhood to handle them.

guised as a suicide, had occurred. The people were genuinely shocked over the incident. The prevalent opinion seems to have been that the young chief had been killed in a drunken brawl; only those (among them Mr. Nowell) who argued that despite appearances it was a suicide connected the death to the ill-fated love affair.

The council of chiefs met to consider the matter, primarily for the reason that they believed that if the agent learned the facts of the case he would very likely regard it as somehow connected with potlatching and hence would take a much more strict stand against the activity. That is, the chiefs specifically disclaimed all interest in the incident as a crime, interesting themselves only in its possible relation to the potlatch. After considerable discussion they reached the following decisions: the death was to be reported to the agent as being from natural causes and the true facts were to be concealed from him. Furthermore, since apparently most of them held to the drunken brawl murder theory of the death, they resolved to put a stop to the roistering of the young people.

This portion of their resolutions certainly would have delighted the agent had he learned of it, for use or possession of alcoholic beverages was prohibited at Fort Rupert and a sundown curfew law obtained for all persons under "middle age"; such persons were not permitted on the village streets after sundown unless accompanied by an elderly kinsman. Breaches of these ordinances were to be punished as follows: offenders against the liquor law would be arrested; the liquor confiscated as evidence; and both offender and evidence turned over to the agent, who could be counted on to take harsh action resulting in both a fine and jail sentence. Violators of the curfew rule would be arrested and fined by the chiefs themselves. It was further provided that if any chief violated these laws or attempted to intervene on behalf of a young relative "all the chiefs would break coppers for [against] him." To enforce these provisions they designated a group of the more responsible young chiefs as a "police committee" of which Mr. Nowell was "chairman." The group was actually a police force, not a committee, but the chiefs apparently liked the English terms, using them without translation. Familiarity with committees, chairmen, and the like derived from missionary-sponsored church groups and clubs and from missionary attempts to set up model village governments. The police committee set up a system of patrols to enforce the curfew law, and arrested at least one offender against the alcoholic beverage ordinance. The unit functioned for a number of years during visits of the tribes to Fort Rupert, eventually breaking up as it became more and more difficult for the Kwagyuł to obtain permission to leave Alert Bay for an extended period en masse.

This anecdote scarcely requires comment, except to point out two things. First, no one, according to the informant, challenged the right of the chiefs to regulate the behavior of their tribesmen; and second, the chiefs' only interest in so doing was their belief that the disorderly behavior, particularly the scandalous case of murder or suicide, would be associated by the Indian agent with the potlatch and would compel him to take more vigorous measures to enforce the law prohibiting that institution.

Several specific instances in which the council of chiefs acted to introduce changes in the potlatch were reported and will be described. They have been referred to briefly in describing historic changes. For example, it must be noted that the action taken by the chiefs of the Kingcome Inlet tribes to put a stop to the use of "checks" in their potlatches represented just such an instance of control of the institution.

On one occasion, in the early years of the present century, the tenaxtəx and the ławitsis were giving a Shamans' Society performance. George Hunt chanced to come to the village in a sloop, on a trading trip, just at the time when a Cannibal Feast was to be given by all the active Hamatsa present. Hunt had "passed through" his Hamatsa novitiate so was no longer active, but he possessed a special privilege in the Kwagyuł rite, that of carving up the corpse at a Cannibal Feast and serving the dancers. As a courtesy he was invited to perform on this occasion and did so. Someone informed on him to the agent. Since Hunt, as well as being *maître d' hôtel* to the Cannibals, trader, and professional ethnographic informant, was Indian constable at the time, the agent was irate. He remitted George for trial before a provincial court in Victoria, placing charges of violation of the "mutilation of human bodies" provision of the anti-potlatch law.[35] Hunt secured counsel to fight the case. Hosts of Kwakiutl appeared as witnesses for him, all affirming that the alleged corpse was no such thing but simply a dummy, and consequently Hunt was acquitted. The chiefs seem to have seen in the affair both a threat and a solution. They met in a sort of super-council in which all the groups resident or near Alert Bay were represented, discussed the matter, and then publicly announced that henceforth only dummies, not real corpses, would be used in the Hamatsa performances and that the biting of flesh from the arms of the living persons would likewise be simulated, not actually carried out. Now the last mentioned act, the biting of pieces of flesh, had always been in part a trick. The Hamatsa, while pretending to tear a chunk of flesh from his victim's arm with his teeth, really shaved off a thin slice with a sharp knife, a procedure which produced a satisfactory flow of blood at the time and later a convincing scar, but was, if moderately painful, immeasurably less severe than actual rending with the teeth would have been. And the bits of skin were not really eaten but were secreted by the dancer to be returned to their owners later. The right to be so "bitten" was a privilege of certain chiefs only and was arranged in advance with the "bitee." It is also a moot question whether real corpses were ever used in the performances or, if they were, whether they were actually consumed or the eating was one of the many stage illusions at which the Kwakiutl were so skilled. These matters, however, have no pertinence in the present connection; the main point here is that from the Indian point of view the chiefs had made a major change in the ceremonial.

About 1926 or 1927, as part of the game of trying to outwit the agent, the chiefs made the change in potlatch procedure that would have rendered the institution unrecognizable to their

[35] This phrase is from the revised antipotlatch and anti-Dancing Society law, in which the offenses were more clearly defined than in the original version.

forebears. This was the "secret potlatch" procedure already mentioned, in which the chief with a small group, including his speaker and secretary, would make the rounds of the houses in the village as unobtrusively as possible, beginning at one end of the village and going from one house to the next in geographic order of the houses, not according to order of rank. At each house the chief stated briefly that a potlatch was being given, by whom, and for what reason. By this time single-family housing units were common. The only recognition of the system of social precedence was that the chiefs of higher rank received the larger gifts. An unforeseen result of this has been that many of the younger people do not know the dances and other privilege displays, nor do they know the real order of precedence of the chiefs. In fact, Mr. Whonnuck asserted scornfully, some of them do not even know their own names—that is, the formal ones associated with the ranked positions—when they attend feasts and potlatches given at the remoter villages.

The control of the potlatch procedures by the chiefs is also amply demonstrated in the institution of the "eagle" (kwik*) statuses. The eagles were persons who participated in the potlatch in the same manner as did the real chiefs, that is, they were entitled to give potlatches and to receive major potlatch gifts. The item that is most striking is that when the distribution of gifts was made in the ancient fashion, in order of rank, the eagles received *before* even the highest ranking chiefs. And yet many of these persons were not chiefs and their positions were dependent on the will of the council of chiefs.

The Kwagyuł tribes of Fort Rupert have a total of twelve eagle positions. The nimqic were said to have either four or six (our data are not clear on this point); most of the other Southern Kwakiutl tribes have these statuses in their potlatch system.

The histories of the eagle positions among the Kwagyuł of Fort Rupert were recorded in detail. In point of fact, in 1953 Mr. Nowell essentially duplicated the account he had given Drucker sixteen years before, in 1937. From these histories it becomes clear that the original incumbents of the positions were for the most part *nouveaux riches*, chiefs of low rank or commoners who wanted to participate prominently in the potlatch and were able to curry favor with the real chiefs so that this special privilege was awarded them. Once created, the positions became hereditary. It may be noted that in no case was there a tradition of supernatural origin of the eagle right comparable to those which substantiated, in the native view, each and every privilege of the real chiefs. All the ceremonial and other rights of the real chiefs were believed to have been acquired by ancestors in the course of supernatural experiences. Recital of the circumstances of origin of such rights, along with an account of mode of transmission to the most recent claimant—via direct inheritance, transfers in marriage repayment, or capture in war—was regarded as the validation of a chief's claim to such a right, comparable in a general way to notarizing a document in our culture. The eagle places had no such origin traditions (although the first of these places to be created depends on an account reminiscent of such traditions). Even the names assumed by the occupants of the places were improvised by the first holders of the titles. Eagle names are high-sounding, sonorous designations referring to wealth and potlatching.

The twelve Kwagyuł eagle places were not created simultaneously but rather were instituted one by one over a lengthy time span. The first of these positions was established in the following manner: There was a chief of the kwɛxa who bore the name nɛmogwis (that of the first ancestor of the namima) who was married to a sister of the chief tsunxqaiyu, the first chief of the walas kwagyuł, and of the namima tsuntsunqaiyu. Nɛmogwis had a son named omaxtalakla'i who was a great hunter. He had inherited a charm, the story relates, consisting of a wad of shredded cedar bark with which blood of the sisiuł —the plumed serpent-lightning monster pet of the thunderbirds —had been sopped up. When he wiped this charm over his sealing harpoon heads, he could not fail to make a kill. The young man killed a hair seal, brought it home, and invited the chiefs to a feast. He invited ma'tagila, first of the kwagyuł, tsunxqaiyu of the walas kwagyuł, his own father nɛmogwis of the kwɛxa, and all the other chiefs. When about to distribute the flesh of the seal he said to his father, "To whom shall I give the breast of the seal?" His father replied, "Give it to your uncle tsunxqaiyu." This he did. Properly he should have given the first cut of the seal to the chief ma'tagila. When he gave the first (and to the Kwakiutl, the most noble) portion to his uncle before giving to the ranking chief of the assembled tribes, he thereby made him the first eagle.

This story does not do much for us in the way of chronological placing. It obviously follows the pattern of the origin legends of other privileges, except for the fact that it does not include the features of supernatural authorization. The item of the sisiuɫ blood charm used by omaxtalakla'i is dragged in by the hair of its head to simulate the literary atmosphere of the supernatural encounter, but does not really put the story on the traditional level. The specific title of eagle comes in as a non sequitur, we may note, to the fact that the hero gave to his uncle out of the proper order. On the other hand, there is nothing in the story that we can pin down as indicating a historic date for the establishment of the place. Mr. Nowell was of the opinion that this was the only really ancient eagle position. Mr. Whonnuck concurred, but as he was the incumbent in recent times of this place, which he had inherited from his mother, his opinion might be qualified as biased.

The position, though it was the first to be established, did not continue in that situation of primacy. A minor chief of the kwagyuɫ married a woman from Kingcome Inlet. In the marriage repayment he was given, or so he said, a copper and a privilege which had been created among the Kingcome Inlet tribes called kotink^w or kotixwuɫta'lak^w, which entitled the owner to be given his potlatch gift before the chiefs were called into the house for the potlatch distribution. He sold the copper and gave a potlatch announcing his claim to the novel privilege.

There is said to have been considerable discussion among the chiefs as to whether or not they should accept this claim. Finally the chief of the kwɛxa gave a potlatch and resolved to recognize the kotink^w right. At that time the guests at a potlatch made a formal en masse arrival at the village of the host, but did not disembark from their canoes until formally invited to do so in order of relative rank. When the guests were assembled in their canoes along the village beach, the speaker of the kwɛxa chief climbed to the roof of the host's house carrying a mink pelt that was to be the potlatch gift. The women of the kwɛxa began to sing and dance. The speaker held up the pelt for all to see and shouted, "We are going to do as the chief of the kwɛxa ordered. The first gift of the potlatch is to be given before you, the guests, are invited to disembark from your canoes. Ko. . . ."

The walas kwagyuł eagle stood in the bow of his canoe, directly in front of the house. He was enraged. When the speaker began to pronounce the term "kotink^w" the eagle produced a musket from under his robe, handed it to a slave at his side, and ordered him to shoot the speaker. The slave did so, and the lifeless body of the speaker rolled from the rooftop before the victim had been able to complete the name of the privilege and that of its holder. The kwɛxa assembled in the house, many of them insisting that the eagle be slain before the potlatch should proceed. The kwɛxa chief, however, took a moderate stand; the walas kwagyuł eagle was a close relative, a "cousin." He invited the other chiefs ashore, to tell them, "My brothers want to kill the walas kwagyuł eagle. They do not want the potlatch to proceed while he lives. But I say that this is wrong. If we kill the eagle, he will die and soon be forgotten. What I say is that it would be better to give first to the claimant of the kotink^w right, making him the first of the eagles in rank and putting the present eagle in second place." The chiefs agreed. Since that time the heirs of the claimant of the kotink^w right have held the first place in the eagle precedence order.[36]

The account of the creation of this place contains several details that aid in giving it chronological definition. One is the mention of the gun used in the slaying of the speaker. This point was discussed at length with Mr. Nowell, since he was the type of informant with whom such matters could be discussed, pointing out that if the murder weapon was a firearm the incident must have occurred in historic times. Mr. Nowell insisted that, in all the renditions of the story that he could recall having heard, use of a firearm was specifically mentioned. He himself

[36] Drucker acknowledges that he confused the whole point of this story in a previously published five-line summary of it (1955:129). The present version is the correct one, as related by Mr. Nowell.

then brought up another time clue, the use of the mink pelt as the intended gift. This item, he said, was also invariably mentioned in the story. To the best of his knowledge of ancient customs, mink skins had no particular value among his people until white traders began to buy them.[37] Negative evidence may be found in the lack of any reference to the Hudson's Bay Company post. Mr. Nowell also commented that the custom of awaiting the formal invitation into the potlatch house in canoes on the beach probably referred to the epoch prior to the formation of the confederated village at the site of the fort, although he admitted that this formality may have been continued for some time after it ceased to be a matter of transportational necessity. Another scrap of negative evidence is the lack of mention of trade blankets; this is not clear-cut, of course, for we do not know how soon the famous blankets began to be used in the potlatch after Hudson's Bay Company began to operate in the region. Taken all together, however, the various internal clues of the account strongly suggest that the incident may have occurred in the period between 1810, when the sea otter trade was dwindling and such traders as did sail to the coast bought whatever furs they could get, and prior to 1849.

The original holder of this highest rank place in the eagle series assumed the name Lakwa (copper). Holder of the position at the time the field data were collected was a man whose English name was Tom Johnson. One of his immediate predecessors acquired, and all have subsequently used, the name o'wɔxalagilis in this eagle place.

The third eagle place was established by the chiefs, third both chronologically and in order of rank, at the time when the ma'amtagila namima of the kwagyuł "went ahead" of the gixsàm. Previously the gixsàm were the highest ranking namima of the "real" kwagyuł. During the period of revision and adjustment of potlatch protocol which apparently followed very soon after the establishment of the Hudson's Bay Company post in 1849, the ma'amtagila claimed that they should precede the gixsàm

---

[37] Mink, marten, and other land furs were purchased by the few white traders who voyaged to the coast after 1810 when sea otter had become scarce.

on the grounds that they were the lineal descendants of the legendary chief ma'atgila, the first and by their interpretation the highest ranking ancestor of the entire kwagyuł tribe. After a time the council of chiefs decided to accept their claim, so that the ma'amtagila chiefs would receive gifts before those of the gixsȧm, but made the following compromise: they created a special place, third in rank among the eagles, for yɛkoLasami, head chief of the gixsȧm, so that he should receive his gift in the potlatch prior to his ma'amtagila rivals. It was said that the bearer of the name yɛkoLasami was "a good chief, and well liked," and for this reason his fellow chiefs made the special place for him. The holder of this title when the data were collected was an elderly man known as Peter Pasquero. The data of the creation of the place can probably be placed as sometime after the formation of the confederacy at Fort Rupert. These three are the oldest eagle places in point of time. All the rest seem to have been created by the chiefs in the latter decades of the nineteenth century and the early decades of the present one.

The fourth, fifth, sixth, and seventh places pretended to antiquity in that they were presented as legitimate claims based on asserted genealogical relationship to the chief tsunxqaiyu, Mr. Whonnuck's ancestor who was the first to have the title of eagle. The fourth place in the ranked sequence was held by a man named Bob Wilson, of whom nothing more was recorded than that he had inherited a place created on the basis of a claim derived as just described. The fifth place in the series was last occupied by a woman called Lakweł. Her mother's mother's father was a chief of low rank of the ma'amtagila who gave many potlatches. He called in the chiefs and told them that he was related to chief tsunxqaiyu because he had married a tsuntsunxqaiyu woman, and that "he would like to have a place among the eagles" (this phraseology is Mr. Nowell's). The chiefs assented, so he gave a potlatch, announcing that he had been given a new place and that his name in the potlatch would be Lakweł. Name and place were inherited by his daughter and then by the woman mentioned, whose son now had the right to inherit the place but has never done so because he has an important status among the Kingcome Inlet tribes.

The sixth place was created by the chiefs for a tsuntsunxqaiyu man incumbent of a very low ranking chief's place in that namima, who gave so many potlatches that when the chiefs potlatched they gave him more than to many persons of higher rank. He too petitioned the chiefs for a place among the eagles, so they created one for him. He used the name làpàlet (Le plet, "the priest" in Chinook jargon) and siwit as an eagle. His son and subsequently his daughter inherited the place. The daughter, xixɛmgilagogwa, died with no close relatives as potential heirs, so this place too has been vacant in recent times.

Captain Jim, hinakyalisu, whom Mr. Nowell recalls as having been an old man when the informant was a youth, had inherited a low ranking chief's position in the gigɛlgam namima of the kwɛxa from his father and through his mother a similarly low place, although still concerned as among the chiefs in the sintȧm of the kwagyuł. Through his father he also had a place in the gigɛlgam namima of the walas kwagyuł.[38] Just how he claimed this relationship was not made clear, but on the basis of this place among the walas kwagyuł he claimed kinship with the holder of the fourth ranking eagle and asked the chief to make an eagle place for him. He made up the name Lakwaigil. The first component of the name is, "copper," the second is suspiciously close to a rendering of the English word "eagle." The informant did not translate the name. His daughter inherited the place, then her son who died without heirs, so that in later years the place has been vacant.

There was a chief of the ya'aixyakami of the kwɛxa who used the name iwɔnuxtsi. He was the first in rank of his namima. His first-born child was a daughter, and he gave a potlatch at which he claimed that she should have the right to an eagle place, with the name hȧmtsid (this name is of Heiltsuk origin; by what right the chief claimed it was not recorded). The chiefs ac-

---

[38] The gigɛlgam were originally a single namima of the walas kwagyuł. The group split into two divisions, and there immediately arose the question of precedence. The "younger" section wanted to outrank the senior one. In pique the latter separated from the walas kwagyuł, joining the kwɛxa tribe. We have no evidence on which to base an estimated date of this incident.

cepted his claim, making the eighth eagle place for hámtsid. The second child born to iwɔnuxtsi was a boy (who acquired the English name Jim Roberts) whom he put in his own place as chief of the ya'aixyakami. The daughter died without issue. Jim potlatched, claiming the place, and his claim was recognized by the other chiefs, so that for the time being he held both an eagle place and that of a real chief. After a time he gave another potlatch at which he put his younger sister's son in the eagle place.

There was a man of the gigεlgam of the kwεxa named puhrdlas, of relatively low rank. He gave a potlatch, at which time he requested the chiefs to recognize his relationship to Chief tsunxqaiyu (via the walas kwagyuł origin of his namima) and to make an eagle place for him. They acceded and he gave a potlatch announcing the fact that he was holder of an eagle place; he took the name ogwilaqami as his eagle name. He had no close kin. When he was dying a ha'aiyalikyawi woman took care of him, and he left his eagle place to her. Her son, Sam Hunt, was the incumbent when these data were collected.

The tenth place was held by a man known as Frank Walker. His mother was a tsuntsunxqaiyu woman who had no place in the potlatch at all (she was a commoner), but she claimed kinship with Mr. Whonnuck (our informant) and with his aid and backing got the consent of the chiefs to give a potlatch, asking that her son be made an eagle (on the basis of the alleged kinship to tsunxqaiyu). So the chiefs made this place.

The eleventh eagle place was made for an adoptive son of Tom Johnson, holder of the first-ranking eagle position. This place was established at the request of Tom's father who was very popular with the real chief.

The twelfth eagle place was made for Bill Cadwalader, George Hunt's sister's son, prominent member of the Fort Rupert community and owner of what is apparently the lineal descendant of the Hudson's Bay Company store. Because of his non-Kwakiutl ancestry, he had no place at all in the potlatch. George Hunt's own lineal descendants inherited his places in the system.

When this last place was made, the chiefs said that they

would not admit any more claims and would make no more eagle places. The ma'amtagila especially were complaining because so many people were receiving prior to them, even though a verbal distinction was made between the eagles and the chiefs; after the gifts had been given to the eagles each in his turn, the speaker said, "la mȧnts naqahoL," "now we go to the real [ones]." Mr. Nowell recalled and gave details of two incidents in which men wanted to acquire eagle places and were unable to do so because of the opposition of the chiefs. Both men gave potlatches (not simultaneously) at which they asserted claims to such rights. One was Mr. Whonnuck's father, who wanted to "share" his son's place (but actually would be acquiring a new place); the other was a kinsman of Frank Walker (eagle number 10). The chiefs presented a united opposition, making it clear that if the claims were pressed they would refuse to recognize them, in both cases hinting that they would, if necessary, potlatch against the claimants. The erstwhile claimants had no recourse but to abandon their claims; they could not possibly accomplish anything by continuing to assert rights that no chief would honor. Not long after Frank Walker's kinsman ran into this impasse the innovation was made whereby the potlatch distribution was made according to the situation of the houses in the village, so interest in the old precedence series waned.

The eagles had no traditional names to assume in connection with the positions, or masks or dances to display. The only thing they could claim was their eagle right awarded them by the chiefs and the made-up name they assumed. The third eagle, the gixsȧm chief, was the lone exception, apparently using his hereditary privileges in his eagle place. One remedy to this situation was to acquire privileges in marriage, using the wealth and such status as attached to the eagle place to obtain a bride of high rank. This is what Mr. Whonnuck's mother's paternal grandmother did when he married the Awikeno "princess." He was the lineal descendant of the original Kwagyuɬ eagle, the one who caused the shooting of the speaker. Included in the repayment of the bride price were a host of privileges, some of which have been mentioned. This man began to use the

Awikeno name doqwais in connection with the eagle place, discarding the improvised name previously used; and his heirs have done the same. They have also made use of the Awikeno grizzly bear performer in the Shamans' Society rites (which enables them to participate in important phases of the performance, something not possible prior to this acquisition) and have staged the dluwulaxa Society performance, a Heiltsuk ritual possessed by only a handful of other Southern Kwakiutl. The institution of the eagles thus might be said to have injected a small measure of social mobility into the otherwise rigid Kwakiutl system.

The Rivalries

The foregoing description of the way in which the chiefs participating in the potlatch exercised formal control over the institution is of interest in itself as an aspect of function, and in addition it sets the stage for treating the topic of rivals and rivalry potlatches.

The rivalry potlatch is highly overstressed in the ethnographic literature, especially in the secondary sources. In all fairness it must be noted that if Boas, who wrote the first descriptive accounts, did not make the function clear neither did he exaggerate the frequency nor the importance of this type of potlatch. Benedict, on the other hand, implies that it was both common and most significant by native standards. This was simply not so, important as the rivalry potlatch may have been to her argument. It has already been brought out, and other writers with firsthand information concur, that, in native eyes and as well as in quantity of wealth goods involved, the greatest potlatch of any Kwakiutl chief's career was the one he gave with the proceeds of the bride-price repayment. In those affairs there was no direct competition with anyone, for the names and privileges announced were those transmitted by the father-in-law to the groom, a transfer which no one could challenge. Nonetheless there were various sorts of rivalries and occasions in which they were given expression in the potlatch. It is well to note a distinction, which we shall use often in the following paragraphs: a rivalry potlatch was one thing; a rivalry gesture incident to a potlatch was another. True rivalry potlatches were relatively few; rivalry gestures, on the other hand, were common and often differed in function.

It should be clear from what has already been said as to the purpose of potlatches that rivalry potlatches could not have been given purely as competitions between two individuals to see who could give away or destroy more wealth goods, as secondary sources occasionally infer. Had such affairs been given, they would not have been potlatches but rather competitive giveaways for which some special name would have to be devised. The one and only purpose of any potlatch was to present before a friendly social unit or units, and more specifically before the chiefs of those units, one's claims to hereditary rights of one sort or another, rights which normally included continued participation in a key role in the potlatch itself. These claims were given the stamp of public approval, that is to say, were validated by the guest chiefs who, when they potlatched subsequently, recognized the claimant by addressing him by his claimed formal name and by giving him a gift in the claimed place in the potlatch precedence series. Barnett spelled this out clearly years ago as a fundamental feature of the potlatch wherever it was practiced, from Tlingit country to the mouth of the Columbia. Failure to understand this one point has been the main factor in the confusion about the potlatch in so many secondary anthropologic sources.

Rivalry potlatches among the Southern Kwakiutl did not revolve about competition for its own sake; they were given to present conflicting claims to a certain specific right or set of rights. That is to say, if two individuals or two social units claimed *the same particular right or rights*, they could give potlatches announcing their respective claims and such potlatches would be rivalry potlatches. At times in cases of such conflicting claims, the decision to accept one or the other, that is, to recognize formally one or the other claimant, was not made casually by the other chiefs, but was resolved by a meeting or series of meetings of the council of chiefs. But even when no such formally reached decisions were made, the final decision represented a concensus of opinion of the chiefs.

We have mentioned in passing an instance of this sort—the one that resulted in the creation of the third ranking eagle place for the gixsâm chief, when the ma'amtagila "went ahead" of the gixsàm in precedence. The ma'amtagila based their claim on a legendary incident that indicated, or at least they maintained that it did, that their original ancestor ma'atagila was the eldest, therefore highest in rank, of all the ancestors of the kwagyuɬ namima. Therefore, they said, they were highest in rank among their contemporaries and should receive first in the potlatches. In other words, they regarded this tradition as historical documentation of their claim to highest rank. This case was then made into a public issue through the mechanism of the rivalry potlatch. The first chief of the ma'amtagila potlatched with the united support of his namima and doubtless with assurances of support from other important chiefs. Before distributing the gifts in his potlatch, he or his speaker recited the traditional incident, stating that henceforth he and his namima should be given potlatch gifts before, instead of after, the gixsàm. The gixsàm chief then potlatched, denying the validity of the ma'amtagila claim. These were real rivalry potlatches. We do not have in our record precise data on the wealth goods given or how many times the conflicting claims were repeated at rivalry potlatches subsequently. We do know, however, that the matter was resolved by the other chiefs of the Kwagyuł tribes, who agreed to accept the claim to precedence of the ma'amtagila but made the special eagle places for the gixsàm chief as a sop for demoting his namima to a lower position.

It appears that in the period following the building of the fort there were more conflicting claims regarding precedence of groups—that is, the namima or even tribes—while toward the end of the century conflicting claims were invariably those of individuals. Another instance of conflicting group claims was recounted. In ancient days, the Kwagyuł tribes, the nimqic, the mamaleleqala, and the ławitsis (the three last named were each single tribes consisting of several namima) formed a "festival unit," feasting and potlatching among themselves but neither inviting nor being invited by other tribes. This was true for some while after the founding of the post at Fort Rupert and the consolidation of the Kwagyuł confederacy. Furthermore, when a Kwagyuł tribe or the confederacy invited, they used to invite only one of the other three tribes at a time; so, as Mr. Nowell put it, "those three tribes didn't know where they stood" in precedence relation to each other. The Kwagyuł had many close ties with the nimqic and have always been especially friendly with them. Eventually the day came when the Kwagyuł did invite both the nimqic and the mamaleleqala. Gifts were given first to the nimqic, then to the other tribe. This was done a number of times. The mamaleleqala objected, saying that they should receive first, and at one affair quarreled violently with the nimqic. Then the rivalry potlatching began. The mamaleleqala invited the Kwagyuł to a potlatch to announce their claim to higher precedence; the nimqic did the same.

In time it became clear that the mamaleleqala were the richer of the two and were "beating" the nimqic. The Kwagyuł chiefs decided to accede to the mamaleleqala claim. But they made one of their compromises: L!akwotlas, the highest ranking nimqic chief, was left the very first place of all, "to show that the nimqic used to be first." He was not made an eagle thereby; he was addressed by his chief name and given his gift as the highest chief of the nimqic. Some of the mamaleleqala objected to this, giving potlatches (potentially these were rivalry potlatches since they involved a disputed claim), but the Kwagyuł chiefs refused to consider any claim to precedence over L!akwotlas. Then the ławitsis chiefs potlatched, claiming precedence over the nimqic, but the Kwagyuł firmly refused to recognize such a claim. From then on when the three tribes were guests the order of giving was: L!akwotlas, as first chief of the nimqic; then the mamaleleqala chiefs; next the remaining nimqic chiefs; and then the ławitsis chiefs. The informant believed that at the time this sequence was established the mamaleleqala did not yet have eagles. Later, when they established a few such places, the order of giving still began with L!akwotlas, then the mamaleleqala eagles, then the chiefs of that tribe, etc.

These two instances are not unique, but were typical of conflicting claims made by groups which led to rivalry potlatching between those groups. The procedures and mechanisms involved are clear enough so that additional comment is scarcely necessary. There is one feature, however, which merits special attention; that was the type of situation in which what we referred to as "potential" rivalry potlatches were given, as when certain of the mamaleleqala chiefs objected to the special post of honor given to the nimqic chief L!akotlas and potlatched, asserting their right to precede him, and when the ławitsis gave potlatches claiming that they should have precedence over the nimqic. These potlatches were in the rivalry pattern but no real rivalries developed, for the chiefs of the Kwagyuł, who were guests at these affairs and received the gifts distributed, were recognized as the final arbiters and let it be known that they intended to stand firm in their decision regarding this intertribal ranking. When they potlatched, they would continue to give to L!akwotlas before giving to any mamaleleqala, and to the other nimqic chiefs before giving to the ɬawitsis. The claimants dropped their claims, no longer giving potlatches to assert them. Once they knew that there was no possibility of getting the formal recognition they wanted, it was pointless to continue. In this the two tribes were in a position comparable to that of the two men previously mentioned who potlatched to claim rights to eagle places in the Kwagyuɬ series, and whose claims were flatly refused.

Individual rivalry potlatches followed just the same pattern as those between groups. They were given to present conflicting claims, and the conflict was resolved not by the claimants themselves but by the guest chiefs. There was only one type of exception to this general statement: what Boas called the "fictitious" rivalries, wherein two chiefs went through the forms of the rivalry contests just to put on an act. Mr. Nowell's father-in-law, the nimqic chief lagyus, staged such an affair—a full-dress potlatch although the amount of valuables distributed was moderate—"against" a ɬawitsis chief, odzistalic. He broke a copper of modest value and ordered a few canoes smashed, which gave spectacularity to the affair. The theme of the affair was the long-dead issue of the attempt of the ɬawitsis to "go ahead" of the nimqic. Afterward the ɬawitsis chief in turn potlatched, asserting the superiority of his tribe, distributing about the same quantity of goods and destroying roughly the same amount of property. "To hear them talk [during the potlatches]," said Mr. Nowell, "you'd have thought that they were really mad at each other. But afterward one would invite the other to eat, and they would laugh over what they had done and plan what they would do later on." Mr. Whonnuck likewise recalled an occasion when he was still a boy, when a kwagyuɬ chief and a mamaleleqala "smashed canoes all along the beach here at Alert Bay." Later he learned that the two were good friends who had agreed to put on a show. Such performances were pure theatrics. The Kwakiutl were fascinated by showmanship; this has been stressed by Drucker (1940, 1955:148–155; 1965:161 ff.) as an important key to the understanding of the Dancing Society performances. Chiefs who realized the entertainment values of such shows and could afford to stage them might put them on. Such affairs, however, were obviously shams, enjoyed but not taken seriously by the people, and were without direct significance to the problem of the functional aspects of the real rivalry potlatch. They might quite properly be compared to class B movies or the less educational variety of television shows in our culture in the relation of these modern shows to our social functioning.

There was another expression of rivalry to complicate the pattern superficially and not really seriously, because this manifestation is easy to sort out from the formal status conflict situation. This is the "hereditary rivalry" case in which traditions of ancestral difficulties set the stage for a very real personal animus between individuals. The personal relationship existing between Mr. Ed Whonnuck and Mr. Tom Johnson is very much to the point. Both of these men were affable, outgoing, and pleasant to strangers. Drucker's contacts with Johnson were very brief, but his opinion is substantiated by statements and anecdotes related by various informants. Yet the two disliked each other intensely. Both had been brought up on the historical tradition previously related of the origin of the kotink^w right and the creation of the highest ranking eagle place, in which that held by Whonnuck's forebear had been relegated to second in importance. Throughout their adult lives neither of them had missed an opportunity to molest or malign the other. *They did not, however, actually potlatch against each other* because it would have been pointless. The eagle precedence was fixed; Whonnuck had no possible legal claim by Southern Kwakiutl folk law which he could present to support a change in his number two eagle status to one higher than that of Johnson. The two men did not, therefore, give full-dress potlatches against each other. What they did was to make what have been called here "rivalry gestures," incidental to real potlatches, the intent of which was to demean, to offend, even to insult the rival without hope of changing the formal status quo.

Rivalry gestures, which will be discussed in detail subsequently, necessarily form a special case. These phenomena were fairly common, incidental to normal potlatching.

Having circled Robin Hood's barn to explain what rivalry potlatches were not, we return to the question of what rivalry potlatches really were. An episode involving Mr. Whonnuck's mother, from whom he inherited second eagle place among the Kwagyuł, illustrates a number of significant points. It may be noted that accounts of this incident were related by both Mr. Nowell and Mr. Whonnuck. The essential facts were the same in both versions; differences were in the explanatory comments that the two informants gave.

Ed's mother's father, as has been stated, was the direct descendant of the original Kwagyuł eagle, since one of his forebears was the man responsible for the shooting of the kwexa speaker in the kotink^w episode. Ed's grandfather had only one heir, the daughter (Ed's mother); and according to the informant Whonnuck, his grandfather made it understood in his later years that he intended that she should inherit his eagle name and place, although he did not formally present her as his heir in a potlatch. He gave various names and other privileges to Ed's father in repaying the bride price, including some of the ceremonial privileges from his Awikeno grandmother, but the eagle place he did not transfer. When he died his daughter gave a mortuary potlatch at which she announced that she was the heir of her father's eagle place and took the name of doqwa'is. For a time she was not active in the place. Her intent was to give a major potlatch to place her son (the informant) in it.

Her father had a kinsman among his paternal relatives who was a "younger brother," who through other relationships had inherited a minor or low ranking place, although still reckoned as a chief's place, in the tribal potlatch order. This individual was actually the closest surviving male relative of the deceased eagle doqwa'is. He therefore gave a potlatch to the kwagyuł, the kwɛxa, the nimqic, and the mamaleleqala in which he announced that he, and only he, was the proper heir to the late doqwa'is, his "elder brother." Henceforth, he said, he would respond when the honorific name "doqwa'is" was called in the potlatches to the chiefs of the kwagyuł tribes and would gratefully accept the gifts given to him in his proper position as second in rank of the Kwagyuł eagles.

Now this was a rivalry potlatch, in the sense that the giver was announcing a claim to rights that he knew perfectly well were contentious. In realistic terms, the "uncle's" legal rights were weakened somewhat at Kwakiutl law because he was not a real "younger brother" of the dead eagle but only a terminological one. Thus his rights as an heir were inferior to those of a direct descendant. His hole card was the generally recognized fact that, as Mr. Nowell put it, "the chiefs did not like to have women [take important roles] in the potlatch." He had given various potlatches in his lower ranking place, demonstrating his solvency and his knowledge of the duties of a chief. He therefore hoped the chiefs would decide the matter in his favor.

Ed's mother, however, had been well indoctrinated in the customs of the potlatch. She in turn gave a potlatch to the several tribes, repeating the assertions of her rights. She demonstrated her knowledge of the traditions by recounting them in detail. Then she ordered one of her father's expensive coppers to be brought out. She paid an important chief of the kwɛxa to bend the copper over just above the "T" and paid other prominent chiefs to mark cuts symbolically with chisels, without actually cutting pieces from the copper. Then she ordered one of her kinsmen to tow it to sea behind a canoe and to cut it adrift in deep water and let it sink. "This is my gift to you, O chief," she said to her rival.

The "uncle" immediately sent for a very valuable copper that he possessed. When his kinsmen brought it from his house, he had the copper cut into pieces in the traditional way, giving fragments to the guest chiefs, except for the "T" or crosspiece, which he nominally presented to his "niece" in unflattering terms, and then went down to the beach to hurl the object into the sea.

Technically the uncle at this stage was ahead on points, so to speak, for the copper he had broken was more valuable than that sunk in the sea by doqwa'is. But then something else happened. "We had a lot of good friends," Mr. Whonnuck said. "Dan Cranmer's people, Charley Nowell's [elder] brother, and a lot of other important chiefs all said they would give my grandfather's real daughter all their coppers and all their blankets, until she made her 'uncle' go broke. Her Nimkish uncle [mother's brother] sent for a very valuable copper he had, saying that he would give it to her if she needed it.

"These things among the Indians," Mr. Whonnuck went on, "are just like white people in politics. It is just like a [white] politician running for election—he has to have a lot of friends so he can get a lot of votes."

While Whonnuck's appraisal may be a bit *simpliste* as far as modern Canadian politics goes, we still like it because it casts light on a crucial point in the resolution of conflicting claims. The announced intent of several important and wealthy chiefs to back Ed's mother resolved the case in her favor. Their avowed reason for supporting the woman was one based on the prior right of a direct descendant over a remote kinsman, even though the former was a female. The informant's statement makes the real reason clear: his mother played a better game of politics. The so-called uncle was beaten at that point; he could not possibly hope to muster enough wealth to compete with the combined resources of the several chiefs, so he simply dropped out of the picture as far as the eagle place was concerned. It would also be naïve to doubt that having friends at court must have been a factor in such cases as that of the gixsȧm chief for whom the eagle place was created; he was "well liked by his fellow chiefs," we were told, and by the nimqic who retained his precedence above the protesting mamaleleqala.

Obtaining and using potent influence in this way was not shady dealing or to be compared with jury tampering in our culture. In Southern Kwakiutl culture it was perfectly correct and really meant that the individual who could count on such support was successful in establishing and maintaining good social relationships with his fellows.

Another rivalry involving a woman occurred at roughly the

same time among the mamaleleqala. The woman was a kinswoman, a couple of generations removed, of Mr. Whonnuck's wife. The male rival was the man whose English name was Amos Dawson, who later on purchased a copper from Mr. Nowell's elder brother for 23,000 blankets. Both were related to a mamaleleqala eagle who had died without direct descendants. The precise genealogical relationships were not recorded, but from informants' comments both of these persons were about equally close according to Kwakiutl reckoning of such matters. On the occasion of the old eagle's death, the woman immediately gave a mortuary potlatch at which she asserted that she was the legitimate heir to the eagle place and the name used in potlatches by the deceased, and that she would henceforth take his place in the potlatch and use his potlatch name. Dawson was not present on this occasion (mortuary potlatches were necessarily spur-of-the-moment affairs, given with little or no advance notice or preparation), and therefore he did not interpose an objection to her claim. This gave the woman claimant a certain advantage according to native standards, for the giving of the mortuary potlatch was normally the obligation of the heir. When Dawson returned to Village Island, the home of the mamaleleqala, he invited the Kwagyuł, the nimqic, and the ławitsis to a potlatch, at which he announced that he was the rightful heir of the late eagle and that he was assuming the eagle name of the deceased and would receive gifts in the eagle place in all potlatches given to the mamaleleqala tribe. Then he distributed gifts to the assembled tribes.

This, again, was a real rivalry potlatch. Dawson was presenting a competitive claim, giving the lie direct to his rival's assertions. In his favor was the fact that he had given a major potlatch on relatively short notice (although with more time for preparation, demanding repayment of debts, and so forth, than the mortuary potlatch given by the woman). Thus he demonstrated that he had the qualifications necessary for the holder of such an important title—that he had or controlled a considerable amount of wealth, and that he understood how to utilize such wealth in the potlatch. Also in his favor was the discriminatory attitude that "the chiefs do not like to have a woman in [a high rank place in] the potlatch." On the negative side he had several points against him. First was the fact that his rival had given a mortuary potlatch. There was a tendency to accept the syllogism that the rightful heir gives the mortuary potlatch; therefore, the giver of the mortuary potlatch is the rightful heir. The second and more significant factor, and one that affected the thinking of a number of the guest chiefs at Dawson's potlatch, was the fact that he already occupied a high-ranking chief's place, with all attendant prerogatives, among the mamaleleqala. There were those among the chiefs who did not consider it proper for a man to hold both an eagle place and a high-ranking place among the chiefs in the same tribal sequence. Mr. Whonnuck's titles, it will be recalled, were in different tribes.

Furthermore, the two were about equal, not only in wealth but in "influence" based on friendships with important chiefs. As a result some of the chiefs favored one and some the other pretender to the eagle place. They could not seem to be able to work out a concerted decision. The affair dragged on for several years. The woman announced that she was going to give a potlatch to prove her claim, one that would make that of her rival seem insignificant, but she never did. Meanwhile, the two contestants resorted to potlatch gestures; that is, at any potlatch to which the mamaleleqala were invited as guests a gift had, of necessity, to be given to a person in the status of the eagle. If the gift were given to the woman, her rival immediately sprang to his feet shouting objections, made a lengthy speech alleging his more valid right to the place, and then destroyed a quantity of wealth goods—throwing blankets or cash into the fire, cutting a piece off a copper, and so on. If the gift was made to the male rival, the woman went through a similar performance. The rival then replied in kind.

It has been indicated in prior discussion that in rivalries the solution as to which of the contestants was to be accepted was expressed in a potlatch in which one or the other was given a gift as incumbent of the embattled status. This present case requires some refinement of that generalization, which can be made by bringing in the factor of "common knowledge." It was generally known that the chiefs of the several tribes who potlatched with the mamaleleqala had not reached an accord as to which of the two rivals was properly entitled to the place. Consequently, if at one potlatch Chief A gave a gift to Dawson as the eagle of the mamaleleqala, everyone knew that Chief B, who was planning a major potlatch a few months hence, was a partisan of the woman's case and would give a gift to her as the proper bearer of the title. So no single gift sufficed to settle the matter.

This particular case had a remarkable denouement, although we hasten to add that this does not negate its validity otherwise as an example of Southern Kwakiutl potlatch rivalry. The two opponents did not miss an opportunity to present their respective cases, using the medium of the potlatch gesture. Mr. Nowell made clear that the case became something of a bore to their contemporaries. Neither could obtain a decisive advantage —they were about equally matched in wealth resources and the knowledge of how to use them in the potlatch. But at every potlatch the two went through their act, which had the same effect as a filibuster on the Senate floor—all progress was halted until it was over. "People got tired of it," said Mr. Nowell, "people would rather receive their potlatch presents than listen to them argue."

The climax came in a potlatch given at Alert Bay. The Indian agent at that time was a former missionary among the Kwakiutl who knew them well and liked them, and is remembered kindly by them. The agent did not then regard the potlatch as being as black and immoral a performance as it was depicted, as long as it was not accompanied by a Shamans' Society rite with its abominable Hamatsa. So he not only tolerated potlatches but even dropped in to watch them as a spectator; he is said to have had a considerable competence in the Kwakiutl tongue.

On this occasion he was observing the proceedings. The giver of the affair was known to be a partisan of the woman competitor for the eagle place, so Dawson came prepared. He had a younger relative smuggle in a very valuable copper under his robe. As soon as the woman was designated recipient of the gift to the eagle position, he proclaimed his objection. He had the copper brought out, related its name and value, and then asked a chief to cut a large piece from its "face" while he himself continued to shout his claims, working himself into a rage—a rightful rage as he saw it, for he was being deprived of something of great value, the eagle title that was "rightfully" his. When the piece had been cut from the copper, he took it and strode forward, shouting that he was "breaking" the copper for the woman. The piece cut from the face he intended to give her, to see if she dared break a copper nearly as valuable. When he stood before her, about to hand her the piece of the copper, she made an insulting remark that so angered him that he hit her in the face with the intended gift and sent her sprawling.

The agent's sense of chivalry was aroused. He hastened forward to reproach the Indian for his ungentlemanly conduct. The latter, however, was too much enraged to brook interference. In fact, the agent's attempted interference gave him a new target on which to vent his spleen. The agent was physically a small man. Dawson towered over him, bellowing, in effect, that the agent should go away to tend his agency and stop meddling in Kwakiutl affairs. The agent glared up at him, replied coldly that if this was the way the Indians were going to comport themselves in the potlatch it was quite time the potlatch was stopped. Then he turned on his heel and went home.

There were many of the Kwakiutl chiefs who were more levelheaded than Dawson. They recognized that this was just the sort of incident that should never have occurred if the potlatching were to continue without interference, or with minimal interference, from their administrator. Their appraisal was correct, for the agent soon began to use all the resources available to him to obstruct potlatching. A meeting of the chiefs was called at which it was decided that this rivalry must be stopped. They resolved to recognize Dawson's claims to the eagle place. The woman claimant was notified that her claims were disallowed and in addition, that she would not be permitted to voice them in the potlatch thereafter.

The factors that seem to have led them to this decision were apparently, first, the attitude that "woman's proper place" was not among the chiefs in the potlatch, and second, Dawson had indicated his intention of placing two different heirs in the two places, thus overcoming their objections to an individual occupying an eagle's and a chief's places simultaneously. Uninfluenced by Tennysonian notions of chivalrous regard for womanhood, the fact that the woman had been physically maltreated concerned them not at all.

This case has some unusual facets, but this does not mean that is was fundamentally atypical of rivalry situations. The point that is of maximum significance to the understanding of rivalries among the Southern Kwakiutl is the way in which the chiefs resolved the competition: They agreed to accept the claims of one of the rivals, meaning of course that in any potlatch any of the chiefs gave from then on they would give to that person as incumbent of the disputed place; and further, as Mr. Nowell specified, they told the "loser," in this case the woman claimant, that *they would not permit her to continue to present her claims during potlatches.* This is the key to the whole matter of potlatch rivalry. This we do not offer as a new interpretation, for Barnett (1938:355, 357) arrived at the same conclusion when he said, "validation of status must come from the other members of society . . . ," and again, specifically referring to rivalry potlatches, "The spectators in this case [the rivalry potlatch] are witnesses. Not only that, they are really judges. They . . . choose the 'winner' and make the final word, which is formal recognition of one or the other of the rivals."

An aspect of the case just recounted requires comment, which, though it may seem to diverge from the course of the main argument, will be shown to be pertinent and necessary to an understanding of the rivalries. Reference is to the displays of ill temper by both rivals each time they were face to face at a potlatch—displays that took the form of angrily shouted denials of each other's asserted claim, insults and threats, and which culminated in Dawson's tantrum. While instances of physical violence were rare in the rivalry situation,[39] verbal expressions

---

[39] The only other instance involving physical violence related by informants was that of the shooting of the kwεxa speaker. There is, of course, the tradition of ancient rivalry involving the chiefs mexhwa and yakodlas, which accounts for the origin of the kwεxa.

of anger were usual. At a casual glance such behavior would seem to fit Benedict's construct of wildly emotional behavior, self-glorification (recitals of one's nobility of lineage), and reckless and random waste of wealth (through distribution and destruction), all for the purpose of augmenting prestige. Her interpretation of Kwakiutl rivalry behavior was manifestly an important factor in leading her to the appraisal of the Kwakiutl culture pattern as "paranoid" and "megalomaniac." That is to say, her final conclusion regarding the Kwakiutl derived in large measure from her own interpretation of the motivation for a common feature of rivalry behavior. However, when we analyze the apparent emotional excesses in terms of what the persons involved were really doing, a very different picture emerges.

In this as in all instances of true rivalry potlatches, neither rival was trying to *augment* prestige through the competitive performances. Each was firmly convinced that he or she was rightfully *possessed* of the specifically rated prestige accruing to a certain social position, that is, each believed himself or herself to be the rightful heir of the deceased mamaleleqala eagle. Formal presentation of a rival claim was consequently regarded as an attempt to deprive an owner of his valued possession. Resentment at an invasion of property right is a normal enough human reaction, so that there is no need to seek an explanation of it in terms of abnormal psychology. Possessiveness, usually accompanied by assumption of an aggressive attitude on occasions of trespass (attempted or accomplished deprivation of a thing possessed), may well be part of the basic psychic equipment of man and even of many lower mammalian forms as well. Among such species of animals that display it, possessiveness is directed to a very few things: sometimes food and perhaps more often the individual animal's own young. Human possessiveness, however, is nearly infinite in its manifestations. It is not necessary to list examples of the myriad items both material and intangible to which the attributes of cultural value and possessiveness have been given. Significant to the present discussion is the fact that the Southern Kwakiutl value system gave special esteem to a variety of qualities and things, and of these the most important of all was hereditary social status. The overt symbols of this status—names, crests, place in the potlatch precedence series, and so on—were, in the abstract, property of the namima; but in specific use they were treated as individual possessions.

In an early portion of this paper we disavowed any intent to discuss Benedict's theory as it relates to the Southern Kwakiutl. We have not switched intentions in midstream; this digression is not meant as a critique of Benedict's hypothesis but rather is intended to clarify our position, which might otherwise have been befogged by the account of the behavior of the two persons in the rivalry situation. Our thesis here is that in its purpose the rivalry potlatch did not differ from the normal affairs. The only peculiarity of the rivalry potlatch was that there were two individuals claiming to be heirs to the same status, so that eventually a selection had to be made by the guests, not the claimants. The tensions and resultant emotional outbursts stemmed from the conviction of each rival that his own claims were just, so that the inheritance was his by right, and that his opponent was trying to take his possession from him illicitly. The very fact that resort to actual physical violence was so rare, despite the very real feeling on these occasions, indicates that even the rages were controlled by culturally defined attitudes; for the Southern Kwakiutl like the Nootkans were strongly opposed to physical violence in any intragroup conflict even though they considered warfare the normal condition in dealing with outsiders.

The fact that it was the chiefs who resolved the rivalry situations in favor of one or the other contender, sometimes by holding a formal meeting to arrive at the decision and sometimes by more casual means, immediately casts suspicion on the "fighting with property" interpretation as the essence of the rivalries. The implication of this phrase is that the rival who gave away and destroyed the greatest amount of wealth was the winner; but the case histories of potlatch rivalries make clear that the host with the most did not automatically get the nod. Had winning one of these conflicts been nothing more than a matter of counting up the numbers of blankets, canoes, and coppers given away and destroyed, there would have been nothing for the chiefs to hold meetings about, nothing for them to decide.

Mr. Whonnuck's opinion as to the royal road to success in rivalry situations having or winning influential friends among the chiefs has been cited. Such friends, he noted, could be counted on to assist a contender in several ways: by lending blankets, coppers, and so forth as needed; by refusing to lend wealth to the rival; and by urging their favorite's case among their fellow chiefs.

Reading between the lines of various accounts of potlatches, both of the normal and of the rivalry varieties, one perceives the suggestion that there was among the Kwagyuł a small clique of chiefs who cooperated closely in all matters relating to the potlatch and whose combined influence was usually sufficient to direct decisions of the council of chiefs. The individuals mentioned by Whonnuck as partisans of his mother's case seem to have been part of such an informal but influential group. Obtaining the backing of such a clique would be the way to guarantee a favorable decision.

Legalistically speaking, a case can be made for degree of closeness of kinship to the previous holder of the contested status as being the most important consideration. This point, however, figured more frequently in the claims of contestants than in the decisions made by the chiefs, because the rules of inheritance were so firmly established that it would have been quite useless for a distant relative of a former title holder to challenge the right of a close kinsman of a dead chief to inherit the status. The case that seems to present such a situation, that of Whonnuck's mother and her rivalry with her "uncle," was complicated by the matter of the sex of the rivals; that is, the "uncle's" contention that, as closest surviving male relative of the deceased eagle his right was stronger than that of a female direct descendant.

Although it did not come into play often, another factor was competence in handling the complex financial operations of the potlatch. The immediate predecessor of Mr. Nowell's elder brother as chief of the kwɛxa in his later years married a widow who had a grown son named lɛkyosa, who was the namima qwu'qwɔ'qwum of the kwɛxa. The Chief o'witi put his stepson in the fourth ranking place of the qwu'qwɔ'qwum. The status was vacant at the time, the last incumbent having died leaving no near kin. A man named nulis, who held a very minor chief's status in the namima, gave a rivalry potlatch at which he announced that he was more closely related genealogically to the ranking chiefly line of the namima and to the past holder of the status than was lɛkyosa, and therefore he, nulis, had a better right to inherit the place. Lɛkyosa potlatched to deny the claims of nulis. The rivalry continued for some years. The claimant nulis "beat" lɛkyosa in potlatches and potlatch gestures, for lekyosa did not manage well. Instead of reserving the blankets he received as potlatch gifts for use in the potlatch and lending them out judiciously to increase his capital, he spent them. He contracted debts that he could not pay. Finally his stepfather Chief o'witi let it be known that he would no longer sponsor lɛkyosa, so the other chiefs decided to let nulis take the place and gave to nulis as the fourth chief of the qwu'quɔ'qwum.

These considerations that affected the outcome of a rivalry situation—kinship, influential friends among the chiefs, and competence at managing potlatch matters—have been discussed in some detail because they bring additional emphasis to the fact that the chiefs controlled and eventually resolved rivalry situations just as they did all other matters concerned with potlatching. We do not, however, imply that there was no element of competition in amount of wealth given and destroyed by the rivals, nor do we mean to say that a marked disparity in quantity of wealth utilized in the potlatch by one claimant as compared with that given and destroyed by his rival was of no significance when the chiefs finally came to a decision on a particular case. The mamaleleqala outdid the nimqic in potlatching, and for that reason the chiefs of the Fort Rupert tribes decided to give the mamaleleqala precedence. But in this situation they insisted on retaining for their friend, the first ranking chief of the nimqic, his original place of primacy. In the case just cited nulis outdid the incompetent lɛkyosa, to the annoyance of Chief o'witi who then pulled the rug from under his stepson. Briefly, there definitely was an effort made to outdo the rival; to succeed in doing so was to gain an important advantage in the contest. What we are trying to do here is to put the quantitative competition aspect of the rivalry potlatch in proper perspective. It was but one of several factors in a contest to inherit a particular social status and associated rights, one which was in broad analysis a contest for the approval of the established chiefs.

The Kwakiutl themselves were fond of emphasizing the quantitative feature of the rivalry potlatches in conversation and in oratory. Even Mr. Nowell generalized on one occasion that "there were two things that were important in the rivalries: one was winning in the potlatching; and the other was having important friends among the chiefs." Later on he developed the theme of the significance of kinship in the rivalry situation as being an additional factor, and his constant emphasis on the control by the chiefs of the rivalries, as of all other aspects of the potlatch, made it clear that he himself recognized that the factor of competitive giving and destroying of wealth was not the whole story. In short, in the generalizations about "fighting with property" we have to do with another of the innumerable examples of the difference between what people say they do and what they really do.

The motivations underlying the interest in the wealth competition which were basic to the competition itself are quite clear. In his discussion of the potlatch complex, Barnett (1938) develops the theme of the significance of the gift to both giver and recipient as a measure of esteem. The totality of the gifts, the total value of the potlatch, is in this sense a public measure of the giver's self-esteem. Barnett's analysis holds good for the Southern Kwakiutl rivalry potlatch as well as for the normal potlatch, but there was an additional factor in the former; for such affairs were regarded as demonstrations of solvency—possession of abundant wealth and/or the necessary combination of good friends and good credit that made it possible to assemble wealth necessary for potlatching. The reason was obvious. An individual who claimed a specific status of chief's rank, with its attendant prerogatives, was simultaneously claiming a permanent participation as a chief in the potlatching. Participation in the potlatch was considered both a right and a duty of the chiefs. Manifestly it would have made no sense for the chiefs to admit to their ranks a person who would not or could not carry out this important function. This then is what a pair of rivals were trying to demonstrate when they strove to outdo each other in giving away and destroying wealth. Each was trying to show that he was financially more competent than his opponent to perform the duties of potlatching which would become his obligation if his claims to the chief's status were recognized.

Kwakiutl logic conceived of rivalries being carried to the point at which one competitor would bankrupt the other. This is what the council of chiefs at Fort Rupert had in mind at the time they prohibited alcoholic beverages and established curfew law, when they announced that if any chief defied their authority "all the other chiefs would break coppers for [against] him," although this would have been a rivalry gesture and not a rivalry potlatch. That is, no one chief could possibly assemble enough coppers to match those possessed by all the other chiefs. The nonconformist would therefore either bankrupt himself or admit to defeat, ignominious in either case because he would have brought disaster upon himself by his disregard of the orders of the chiefs as a group. Actually the cases recorded indicate that as a rule rival claimants who contested the right to inherit a particular status were fairly evenly matched financially. Lɛkyosa, of the last case cited, was one of the exceptions. That unfortunate found himself in the position of having limited capital of his own, and then, his stepfather's support withdrawn, he could no longer expect to be able to borrow from his stepfather or from the latter's wealthy friends. He was, therefore, practically in bankruptcy, but it was as much his stepfather as his rival who put him in that unhappy situation.

The Rivalry Gesture

What is designated here as the rivalry gesture was quite distinct from the rivalry potlatch in both form and motivation. In form, it involved the presentation or destruction of a single item or a single lot of wealth goods to embarrass, belittle, or offend some person toward whom the maker of the gesture bore ill will. Such a gesture was properly made during a potlatch, that is, on a public occasion. The maker of the gesture could be, but did not have to be, the giver of the potlatch. He might be in a guest status at the affair or, if he were involved in a case of conflicting claim to a specific status (engaged in potlatch rivalry), might be present but omitted from the list of persons of status. When chiefs and eagles whose statuses were established performed these acts, they did so with no intent of altering their own or their opponent's formal status. The rivalry gesture gave the individual toward whom it was directed two alternatives: to make a comparable gesture in terms of value of the goods given or destroyed or to accept what was regarded as humiliation and defeat.

The Indians equated these gestures with rivalry potlatch situations principally because coppers were often used—that is, broken—and the coppers were regarded by the people themselves as an integral part of the potlatch complex. At the same time they drew a clear distinction between the two forms. For example, there was no formal action taken by the other chiefs; if one of the rivals bested the other he got nothing out of it comparable to the reward achieved by the winner of a contest to inherit a specific status. All he attained was whatever satisfaction he might find in having embarrassed his opponent and in having given the tribal gossips something to roll their tongues over for a long time to come. The "loser" suffered a blow to his pride which he could salve by planning a gesture in revenge at some later date. He continued to attend potlatches and to accept his proper gifts in his proper place in the precedence list. It was wise, though, for him to talk softly and little lest his opponent taunt him publicly. It must be added that cleancut "wins" were few and impermanent. An apparent "loser" bided his time, until he could make an even more spectacular gesture. And the animosity grew.

The usual form the rivalry gesture took in our informants' lifetimes was the destruction of wealth goods as indicated. Usually it was a copper that was broken, but other things of value might be destroyed: canoes smashed or blankets, money, or quantities of olachon grease thrown into the fire. At an earlier time the gestures sometimes took the form of a splendid gift to the rival, which he had to match or better in order to save face. Mr. Whonnuck recalled a little moral yarn his father used to tell him about a cynical Kwagyuł chief who used to visit the niwiti, ostensibly on trading trips. This was at a time before the niwiti potlatched with the Kwagyuł tribes, when they and the Blunden Harbor people and possibly the goasila had their own separate potlatch group. This chief, on his visits, invariably made up insulting songs to sing to his hosts. One went, "I have my foot on the necks of the niwiti chiefs." The niwiti, incensed, deluged him with sea otter hides, coppers, and other valuables. "They beat him, my father used to tell me," said Mr. Whonnuck, "but he [the cynical chief] didn't care because he got all their property." Since the niwiti were in a different potlatch group their opinion of him concerned him not at all.

The informant's father understood the point of his own story quite well. On one occasion a haxwɔmis chief broke a copper, giving him the T-shaped central crosspiece, the most valuable portion always reserved for the principal "enemy." Some time later the elder Whonnuck tied the crosspiece to a copper of his own, even larger and more valuable, and had the two objects taken out in a boat to a point well offshore to be "drowned," i.e., dropped over the side in deep water. This he did, Mr. Nowell pointed out, to make sure that his own gesture could not be of any benefit to his rival. Had he broken the copper and given the haxwɔmis the cross piece, the latter might have sold the fragment privately to someone interested in assembling the fragments of the copper, riveting them together to start the object on a new cycle. The crosspiece of a copper valued at several thousand blankets could be sold for at least a thousand, enough to give the haxwɔmis valuable assistance toward the purchase of another copper which he could break for his opponent.

This particular animosity went back to some petty squabble a generation earlier. It continued to a third generation, for the informant and the son of the haxwɔmis chief have carefully cultivated the strained relationship. On the occasion of the mortuary potlatch given at the death of a daughter a few years prior to Drucker's 1953 visit, the haxwɔmis man cut a large piece from a copper and threw it into the sea. He did not say for whom he performed this act, but the informant felt sure that he himself was intended as the object of this unkind attention and that sooner or later his foe would make the fact public. In preparation, Mr. Whonnuck collected some debts of olachon grease owed to his deceased father-in-law, made and purchased a good deal more, and purchased a copper named L!asaxilaiyu for four hundred and twenty-five cans of grease (valued at $15 per can). "I'm reserving the copper for him [the rival] in case he ever mentions me [in connection with the broken copper]," Mr. Whonnuck said, then added, with affected casualness, "It's up in the attic, somewhere, now."

The procedure of breaking a copper without making clear at the time for whom the insult was intended was not standard practice. It might be done, as seems to have been the case in this instance, as part of a war of nerves by a chief who sustained formal animosities with several individuals, each of whom would assume the gesture had been meant for him. It was not specifically reported, but there were probably several coppers sequestered in as many different attics awaiting the haxwɔmis man's announcement of his intention, and hence a sizable amount of potlatch capital immobilized.

Ingenuity seems to have set the only limits on devices for embarrassing others in these gestures. When Whonnuck's father drowned the big copper for the haxwɔmis chief, he had the piece displayed by one of the young men of his namima and, holding his speaker's staff, calmly and dispassionately recited the object's history and value. Then, without indicating for whom he was doing it, he called on Chief sisahwɔlis to bend the copper over just above the cross-piece, the usual preliminary to cutting pieces from it with a chisel. Sisahwɔlis suspected what was coming, but could not refuse. It was a chief's duty to comply with such a request. When he had bent the copper double, the owner produced the cross-piece given him by his rival, tied it to his own double copper as related, and ordered the two pieces "drowned"—for the father-in-law of sisahwɔlis. The latter, enraged, vowed revenge, but seems never to have made good his threats.

An instance of a more subtle kind of rivalry gesture was one made by Mr. Whonnuck in 1932. His arch foe, o'wɔxalagilis, the first eagle of the Kwagyuł, had made public his intention of giving a flour feast. It even became known that o'wɔxalagilis made up a song to use at the occasion, the burden of which went, "All the rest [i.e., of the eagles and chiefs] are asleep." The year 1932 was, after all, still in the depression era. Potlatching, like many other luxury activities the world over, was at low ebb.

O'wɔalagilis had ordered one thousand sacks of flour from the local store owned by Dan Cranmer and Moses Alfred (both Kwakiutl). The partners had received notice by mail that the flour would be on the manifest of the following sailing of the coastal steamer from Vancouver when o'wɔxalagilis informed them that he intended to pay only one-fourth of the price of the flour on delivery and the balance at some unspecified future date. This left the merchants less than happy. They approached Whonnuck with their problem. Undoubtedly they did so because they saw the hereditary rivalry situation as made to order to help them get rid of the flour for cash.

Mr. Whonnuck prefaced his account of the incident with the words, "In 1932 we took a firm stand on the potlatch." This was, of course, partly rhetoric for what he really meant was that he had taken a firm stand on his "rivalry" relationship with o'wɔxalagilis. He had sufficient cash on hand in his potlatch funds which he had been keeping for use on some suitable occasion, so he bought the flour. He made arrangements to give the feast in his wife's uncle's house on Village Island, using various dishes and names that had been given to him in the marriage repayment. One reason for this choice of locale was that he knew that his foe intended to give his feast at that place, since the latter had blood relatives there. O'wɔxalagilis managed to assemble between four and five hundred sacks of flour from other sources, so that he gave a flour feast after all, even though a smaller one. But Mr. Whonnuck considered that he himself had scored a major victory in giving his feast with the flour his opponent had ordered but had not been able to pay for. That aspect of the situation was common knowledge among the Southern Kwakiutl within a very short time after Whonnuck made his decision to buy the flour ordered by the storekeepers for o'wɔxalagilis.

Potlatch gestures were numerous. The field notes contain many other instances, but it is not necessary to relate them all since they all conform to the pattern described here: all were characterized by a lively animosity; and all were aimed, some subtly and some crudely, to embarrass an opponent publicly. Many originated in direct personality clashes of the persons concerned; others were "hereditary" in the sense that some conflict between ancestors was recalled, resentfully, so that the descendants regarded each other with active dislike.

To summarize this topic, there can be no doubt that the rivalry gesture—it might even be better to designate it the "animosity gesture"—was something completely different from the potlatch, although it was normally performed in the potlatch setting. We have stressed that the potlatch was socially an integrative force. Even the rivalry potlatch, although it seems to have deviated from that norm, can be viewed as integrative in the long run; for it was part of a mechanism through which conflicting claims to inheritance of a certain social position were clarified and eventually resolved—once the chiefs reached their decision, no further dissent or conflict was permitted. The rivalry gesture, however, was conflict in the essence. It was even more; it was intragroup personal conflict such as may occur in any society, channelized by cultural norms. The most reasonable explanation seems to lie in the fact that the Southern Kwakiutl cultural attitudes, while favoring war as the normal state where outsiders were concerned, strongly abjured physical violence in intragroup situations. Within the group—namima, tribe, and even confederacy—murder and mayhem were of rare occurrence. In this respect as in so many others, the Southern Kwakiutl and their Nootkan neighbors were culturally alike. Hence it seems reasonable to regard the rivalry gesture as a culturally approved release mechanism for the interpersonal tensions that may be generated in any fairly complex "primitive" society.

In terms of culture concepts the rivalry gesture appears to be derived, as Barnett pointed out, from the so-called face-saving potlatch. However, full-dress potlatches were rarely given by any group for this purpose, except in ancient days when a person of high rank had been captured in warfare, then ransomed from the enemy. According to potlatch etiquette among all groups sharing the potlatch complex, whenever a person of high rank suffered a slight or other indignity, whether accidental or intentional, on a public occasion (which meant, of course, during a feast or potlatch) he had to make a gesture involving either the giving or destruction of wealth. As a rule the gesture, quantitatively speaking, depended on whether the mishap or slight was regarded as an accident or an intentional insult. A chief who stumbled as he entered the potlatch house redeemed his dignity by giving a blanket to his host, unless he believed some malevolent charm had been invoked to make him appear ridiculous, in which case he would make a more spectacular gesture. The Southern Kwakiutl, of course, shared this custom with their coastal neighbors. At their feasts quantities of olachon oil might be poured on the fire to make it blaze hotly, as a deliberate, heavy-handed practical joke. Both Mr. Nowell and Mr. Whonnuck made clear that they regarded this situation as a humorous one. Chiefs seated nearby, who could not stand the discomfort and moved from their places, had to make a face-saving gesture which usually took the form of throwing wealth —blankets or money, but in moderate amounts—on the fire "to put it out." If, however, the butt of the joke was a chief who was in open enmity with the feast-giver, he would throw in a considerable amount of property and perhaps even a copper. The feast-giver would respond by having great quantities of oil poured on the fire or putting a canoe on it to burn. Otherwise, the amount destroyed was nominal. Mr. Whonnuck remarked on one occasion, "Feasts cause lots of problems; sometimes I think they are more difficult than potlatches. Take my tsonoqwa dish, for example, I have to be careful how I seat the chiefs to eat from it, because no one wants to eat from the hind end. [Certain anatomic details of the tsonoqwa are depicted with what may be called "considerable vigor."] If I seat a chief there, he will get up and throw some blankets into the fire or maybe promise a feast, or even a potlach. That's why we usually get together beforehand to plan what we are going to do."[40]

Given the concept of the face-saving gesture, the rivalry gesture becomes meaningful. One of the two individuals concerned felt himself publicly affronted, in which case a face-saving gesture was the proper move to wipe away the stigma. Existence of real ill will gave motive for trying to make the face-saving gesture simultaneously one that might discomfort or embarrass the offender, who then found himself insulted and replied in kind. In the case of the hereditary rivalries, gestures of this sort were commonly triggered by deliberate and impolite reference of one of the rivals to his own ancestor's victory over the predecessor of his rival. If the first-ranking eagle of the Kwagyuɫ, for example, stressed the fact that his superior rating in the procedure list was attained when his ancestor caused the demotion of the man who formerly had been the first of the eagles, he could be sure that Mr. Whonnuck, descendant of the demoted eagle, would break a copper to display his resentment of the taunt to save face and at the same time to try to embarrass his hereditary opponent.

---

[40] The last statement is an allusion to the fact that sometimes what appeared to be affronts were planned with the acquiescence of the person to be "affronted," if, for example, the latter was planning to give a feast and wanted a dramatic way to announce the fact. Such connivance was especially common during the "Winter Dances" (cf. Boas, 1897:343).

The Verbalization of Conflict in the Potlatch

An important part of Codere's thesis relating to the potlatch is the concept expressed in the title of her study, *Fighting with Property* (1950). That is to say, she derives not the origin of the complex, but its principal historic period stimulus, to the warfare pattern. She develops the theme that the potlatch came to serve as a substitute for native warfare, as a prestige activity when native warfare was abruptly and forcibly stopped by British authority. To this end she stresses the expressions of conflict in potlatching and, in a final section of her book, presents a discussion of metaphors referring to warfare used in the potlatch.

We disagree. That is to say, we regard the interpretation as to the primary significance of warfare in connection with the potlatch as in error, although there is not the least doubt that war concepts had some importance in the complex. Perhaps we should say that we disagree in an incomplete way, or else that we are in very limited agreement. We consider the "fighting with property" interpretation as a construct that is not quite in accordance with the basic facts. What is particularly interesting about the situation is that the construct is not, as so often happens, a synthesis developed by an anthropologist, but is a construct formulated by the natives themselves.

In support of our view we note the following points: The "fighting with property" did actually figure in real rivalry potlatches; but as we have brought out, it was but one of several factors concerned in the resolution of the competition of the disputed inheritance in each case and was not the most important of these factors. The Indians, nevertheless, were very fond of rolling the phrase over their tongues, an aspect of the problem that we shall enlarge upon a bit further along in our argument.

"Fighting with property" was essentially what was involved in the rivalry gestures—or "animosity gestures," a designation which we like better—but we have demonstrated that these gestures, although made in the setting of the potlatch, differed in function and significance from both the normal and rivalry potlatch.

The fictitious rivalry potlatches have an important bearing here. Their existence clearly proves that the rivalry situation appealed to the native sense of the dramatic. It is also noteworthy that even these affairs were not staged as competitions merely for the sake of the competition, but were given a specific, if imaginary, target, as in the case of Chief Iagyus and the ławitsis chief pretending to be fighting out the ancient and long resolved issue of nimqic versus ławitsis precedence. Even the fictitious rivalries did not pretend to be solely endeavors to give away or destroy the most wealth but were related to a specific issue regarding status. This point is highly significant in relation to the real rivalry potlatches, clinching our point that they were for specific statuses, not competition merely for its own sake.

Codere cites numerous examples of oratorical references to warfare in connection with the potlatch: war, fighting, and blood pouring over the ground. There is not the least doubt that the Southern Kwakiutl were fond of spectacular and picturesque figures of speech, particularly but not exclusively in oratory, and that they seized upon the symbolic parallel of the competition in true rivalry situations and warfare as a source of metaphor. The question is just how literally should this verbalizing in military terms be taken. Obviously all their speeches cannot be taken at face value; they talked of spilling their "rivals'" blood with one breath and referred to them as "our friends" in the next. And in speeches just as formal and flowery, the "rivals" or "friends" through their principal chiefs, thanked their hosts for their gifts, for explaining the facts concerning their hosts' high rank, and so on.

Some of the references to warfare derived from references to the Shamans' Society performance must be distinguished from those properly related to the potlatch. The Winter Dance had a more direct specific connection with warfare, dramatizing the acquisition of supernatural power from spirits giving war powers, although other types of spirit powers were also represented. A similar qualification must be noted in regard to the names of coppers noted by Codere as having warfare connotations. There were many coppers with names of that type. But there were also many coppers whose names had no reference whatsoever to war. Codere mentions some such in other parts of her study: "Moon"; "Sea Lion"; "Long Top"; "To-clean-everything-out-of-the-house" (Drucker translated this name, "na'mu'-magwila," "Empties-the-house [of wealth]"); "All-other-coppers-are-ashamed-to-look-at-it"; "Looking below" (in order to find blankets with which to buy it). Other important coppers had names such as li'ta, "Searches out [all the wealth]"; lobiʇila, "Sweeping away [wealth]"; L!ahwulamis, "Steelhead trout" in Heiltsuk; ga'wi, "Raven" in Heiltsuk. In other words, even the coppers, which played important parts in actual competitive situations, were not given names referring exclusively to war. As a matter of fact, coppers had an even more important functional relationship with marriage than with "warfare" (rivalry) situations, as we have indicated; while jokesters may correlate the two institutions in our culture, there is no evidence that there was a comparable association in Kwakiutl civilization.

To return to the basic matter of metaphor, there is considerable reason for believing that not only the picturesque references in the speeches to head-taking and to blood and slaughter, but also the milder references to rivalry and competition in formal address, should not be taken literally in every case. The speeches recorded by Boas in connection with the 1895 ceremonials and related potlatches involving the Kwagyuł and the kosqimox, cited by Codere, are a case in point. The pep talks at the secret meetings of the Kwagyuł chiefs (or as Mr. Nowell would have said, "the council of chiefs") regarding efforts to "avoid being beaten by the Koskimos" are scarcely to be taken at face value. Potlatches were not arranged on the spur of the moment. Such additional affairs as were given must have been planned for a long time previously. The pattern described by Boas, regarding the accumulation of wealth, strategically loaned out long in advance to build up a capital to use in a potlatch, is in accord with both specific statements as to potlatch planning and cases cited by all informants consulted for data of the present study, except that our informants consistently indicated that usually a number of years, not just a single year, was normally involved in planning and financing such an affair. Codere (1961:468–469) documents this point amply in her discussion of Cranmer's potlatch record book: "Daniel Cranmer's preparations ran from 1913 to his potlatch in 1921" (p. 469). What the purported "pep-talk" style of speech actually must have been intended for was to give any chief known to have been planning to potlatch on the occasion the opportunity to make a formal announcement, dramatically, to that effect. We are reading between the lines here, for Boas did not ask pointed questions to find out what was going on, but rather accepted what Hunt recorded or reported to him. We do know, however, that not only the Southern Kwakiutl but other neighboring groups on the coast went through some rather elaborate machinations to set the stage for "surprise" announcements of potlatches and feasts. Thus while we cannot prove the point, we feel there are valid grounds for believing that the alleged "rivalry" between the Kwagyuł and the kosqimox was just another dramatic device, not an actual incentive to bigger and better potlatches.

The same applies to the phrasing of the "pairings" of the Kwagyuł with the associates of their ancient festival group. Our informants expressed the pairings as rivalries (as Hunt did for Boas): the kwagyuł (gwɛtala) "versus" the mamaleleqala; the kwɛxa "versus" the nimqic; etc. It appears, however, that all the pairing really meant was that formerly, in the days of the smaller scale potlatches and limited guest group, one tribe invited *only* one other. The kwagyuł thus customarily invited only the mamaleleqala, not the nimqic or ławitsis. There are no details whatsoever indicating any actual competition between them. In brief, this was just another example of the fondness of the Kwakiutl for using metaphors referring to war and rivalries as a part of their liking for picturesque figures of speech which cannot be taken literally.

To sum up this topic we offer the interpretation that the verbal references to war and rivalry in the potlatching was principally a matter of style. Actual potlatch rivalries and the rivalry (animosity) gestures were expressions of conflict. They were, however, intragroup conflict situations or competitions. Their interpretation in terms of warfare means that they were described in terms of intergroup conflicts. A substitution of meaning was involved, and this, we argue, was clear to the Indians; so that such verbalizations, while interesting and enlightening in terms of native thinking, must be taken with the proverbial grain of salt.

The Mortuary Potlatch

A brief résumé of procedures during the Southern Kwakiutl mortuary potlatch was given by Mr. Nowell incidental to a discussion of other matters, and various comments referring to such affairs were made by both principal informants. Drucker intended to explore the topic more thoroughly but somehow never got back to it. The data, sketchy as they are, will be presented; for while this variety of potlatch has been overshadowed in most previously published accounts by more spectacular performances, it was manifestly of great social significance to the Southern Kwakiutl themselves, and of theoretical importance as well in pointing to a greater degree of similarity in formal aspects of the potlatch between Southern Kwakiutl and northern non-Wakashan-speaking groups (Tlingit, Haida, Tsimshian) than is sometimes assumed. Wike (1952:100–101) touches on the relationship of potlatching to attitudes toward the dead in the area in general: the problem merits further analysis if sufficient information on it can be assembled.

Our data do not specify just how soon after the death of a chief the mortuary potlatch was given, but internal evidence suggests that it took place some days after the chief's demise, after the initial period of rigorous mourning. During the first few days the close relatives, that is the members of the namima and other individuals who regarded themselves as close kin, assembled morning and evening in front of the house to wail and to sing dirges. Other people might assemble to watch but did not participate. Aside from the problems imposed by mourning restrictions, organizing a potlatch required a certain amount of time and preparation. It may be noted in passing that the northern mortuary—memorial is perhaps the better word— potlatches actually consisted of a series of steps: the wake; the burial (formerly cremation); preparation of the memorial pole (nowadays ordering, receiving, and setting up the tombstone); and so on, so that the real potlatch might not take place until a year or two or even more after the death, although the whole sequence is regarded by the Indians as one single procedure.

When the time came the heir of the deceased called in the guests. The dirges of the namima were sung, and apparently the guests joined with the hosts in the singing. Following this was a eulogy of the dead chief in the form of a song composed at the request of the heir. This song, called saaligi', listed all the feasts and potlatches given by the deceased, the names of the coppers he had sold to give potlatches, and the names of the coppers he had broken. Then, if the deceased had been breaking a copper for some rival, the heir would have the copper brought out, and cut another piece from it to present to the rival as an indication that he intended to continue the enmity. Such a piece of copper was referred to as a "bone of the dead chief." It might not actually be given to the rival, but rather thrown on the floor to be picked up by some poor man so that he could sell it privately. This was done often when a good many pieces had been cut from the copper. The part that remained, including the valuable cross-piece, was thus tossed out in defiance of the enemy, to be recovered by some commoner. Both Nowell and Whonnuck insisted, however, that they had been told that long before their day one or more coppers were cut into strips, called "the bones of the dead chief," and distributed to the guest chiefs without any implication of challenge or animosity, a usage which exactly duplicates one performed by most or all Tsimshian divisions in olden days. When Mr. Whonnuck's mother gave the mortuary potlatch for her own father she had a valuable copper "towed" out offshore to be sunk in deep water. The informant asserted that this act had been performed to demonstrate her grief, not as a rivalry gesture to anyone. Her uncle had not yet come forward to challenge her heritage; the copper which she "drowned" as a gesture against him was a different one. The dirges were repeated, and then in a sort of chant the guests asked, "Which way has he [the dead chief] gone?" A dancer appeared, wearing the mask representing the original ancestor of the namima of either the father or the mother of the deceased. The ancestor symbolized by the mask indicated which "way"—that is, whether to the paternal or maternal line—the deceased had gone to resume the form in which the first ancestor on that side has appeared.

After this, in the nighttime, came a phase of the performance known as q!italaɬa, translated as "to shake off sorrow." At this time various display privileges—masks, songs, and dances—belonging to the deceased and being transmitted to his heir were performed. As a rule these consisted of rights in the Winter Dances which were displayed in abbreviated form. Usually these were from the Shamans' Society rites, although in relatively recent times, after a number of chiefs had acquired dluwulaxa privileges from the Heiltsuk, these might be shown instead. Performances from both Dancing Societies, if the chief had rights in both, could not be used on the same night. Finally, gifts were given to the guests and the affair concluded.

Socially speaking, the significance of this whole rite was the heir's presentation of himself in that capacity, that is, formally claiming the rights to inherit all the ceremonial and other prerogatives of the deceased chief, in many cases even the enmities. In normal cases, that is when no opponent emerged to challenge his claim to be rightful heir, this was all he needed to do to establish his social position—not to "acquire" status, but to accept that which was his due. Thenceforth he would attend potlatches to which his namima or tribe was invited, be addressed by the host by the name borne by his predecessors in that noble status, and be given his potlatch gift at the place in the precedence series to which his hereditary status entitled him.

Conclusion

As we have presented our data and discussions, we have tried to develop the thesis defined in the early pages of this paper: that the potlatch of the Southern Kwakiutl in its social functions, economics, and mechanics conformed to the basic pattern of the complex in the area, as clarified in Barnett's (1938; n.d.) studies. Features previously regarded as anomalous may be seen on analysis to resolve into expressions of areal patterns or, as in the case of the infinitely compounding double return, prove not to have been actual native custom. The true rivalry potlatch, which has been interpreted by others as being socially disintegrative and even as a manifestation of psychic abnormality, we have shown to be basically a technique for resolving conflicting claims of presumptive heirs. In a broad sense, it was simply a process at civil law. It likewise provided a channel for emotional release by the parties in conflict. To let off steam in controlled surroundings appears to have made possible the preservation of a very important behavioral value standard, one that strongly opposed intragroup physical violence in conflict situations. The rivalry gesture seems to have operated consistently as the same sort of a release mechanism. Our position, therefore, is that these specializations of the potlatch complex were not significant as deviants from the areal norms. One might even interpret them as highly consistent with the fundamental function of the institution, that toward social integration.

Motivations

The potlatch did not give, or create, social status. Present data make abundantly clear that this was as true of the Southern Kwakiutl as it was of other northwest coast groups. No matter how many potlatches a chief gave, he did not alter his formal rank one whit beyond that to which he was legally entitled through heredity or acquisition of rights in marriage. For example, although Mr. Whonnuck derived great satisfaction from his performance in the flour feast episode and regarded it as a moral victory, he did not thereby alter his formal status vis-à-vis his arch rival; In any potlatch given in the old fashioned manner, in which the precedence order was signalized, Mr. Johnson, o'wɔxalagilis, would still be the first of the Kwagyuł eagles to receive a gift, and Mr. Whonnuck would remain in second place. And it was precisely the precedence order that was of most importance in the Southern Kwakiutl social system.

The misconception so often encountered in anthropological literature that an Indian gained social status by potlatching, or potlatched to gain social status, comes in part from the Indians themselves; it is thus one of the categories of ethnographic fact mentioned in earlier pages, what people say they do. The Southern Kwakiutl and their neighbors as well liked to say, in effect, "So-and-so was a great chief because he gave many potlatches." Close analysis reveals that the reverse was actually true: So-and-so gave many (read "several major") potlatches because he was a great ("highly ranked") chief. The distinction between *acquiring* status through potlatching—the popular misinterpretation—and *confirming* or *validating* hereditary status is not a minor one. It is crucial to the understanding of the whole system. The only exceptions to this rule, and they were few indeed, were those who in relatively recent times, by potlatching and by otherwise establishing good personal relationships with the chiefs, were able to persuade the chiefs to create eagle places for them. And even these eagle places once established had a precedence order that no amount of potlatching could change.

At the same time it must be specified that reference is to the formal structure of hereditary status and rank, the precedence order of the occupants of the seriated positions in the namima and tribal role systems. Quite apart from this, there did exist a factor of informal prestige inextricably linked to potlatching; the key word here is "informal." Interest in this factor had a motivational significance affecting individual behavior. This informal prestige is essentially the element that Barnett (1938: 354–355; n.d.:95–100) refers to as "esteem"—the self-esteem of the potlatch giver and the esteem accorded him by his guests.

Barnett's analysis both puts the "esteem" or informal prestige feature of the potlatch in proper perspective in relation to the formal social structure, and develops the theme of its significance as an incentive to the individual (particularly in n.d.: 95–100). We accept his conclusions on this matter; what we shall do here is to draw on our Southern Kwakiutl data to sort out some of the major constituent forces of the "esteem."

First of all, occupying the conspicuous position of giver of the potlatch was a source of ego gratification, especially since so doing implied recognition of hereditary right, which was to the Kwakiutl the highest value of all. One does not have to be a megalomaniac to respond pleasurably to such recognition. The flowery speeches of gratitude by the guest chiefs were designed to heighten this effect. As Barnett has pointed out, the guests on their part received a complementary gratification in the host's recognition of their statuses, not only by his gifts but by his adherence to the rules of precedence in giving and use of the guests' formal titles.

Another element of the self-esteem was obviously the solid satisfaction any person in any culture finds in the adequate performance of the duties of his social role. The data emphasize that the Indians regarded potlatching as an obligation of the chiefs. They were quite aware than a potlatch did not just happen, like spontaneous combustion. A potlatch was staged properly only after long and careful planning, not only in the assembling of the wealth goods, notifying debtors, decisions made as to the amount to be given to each guest, and other financial details arranged; but the privileges to be shown had to be selected, ceremonial paraphernalia refurbished, dancers rehearsed, songs made and taught to the singers, speeches planned, arrangements made with fellow chiefs regarding their participation, the invitation party organized and dispatched, and a host of other preparations made. The chief did not do all these things himself; like any good executive he delegated them to his namima brothers and fellow tribesmen. But he had to see to it that all these things were tended to. (Reference is to a chief potlatching in his own right, not a youngster whose potlatch was really managed by his father or other elder relative.) Giving a potlatch, in short, was a demonstration of a certain administrative competence. This was the work of the chiefs, as the Kwakiutl would say. A man who accomplished all this had a right to a certain pride in his performance.

Another complex of factors involved the subtle nuances in gift-giving, a subject explored in considerable detail by Blau (1964:106–114). In broad terms the potlatch giver publicly and conspicuously affirmed or reaffirmed his position relative to his peers, and that relative to his inferiors, at the same time that he distributed valuables to gain the good will of his guests (normal amicable situations are being discussed here; rivalry gestures are in a different category). That this sort of situation is emotionally rewarding is obvious.

A final motivational factor with strong derivative satisfactions to which we invite attention is what has been called "gamesmanship." This was certainly a major constituent of the rivalry gestures, particularly in the case of the hereditary rivalries, although it was also a factor in the true rivalries. In the latter, however, the aggressive-defensive reaction previously discussed as a result of the invasion of right was the major motivating factor.

It is clear also that these several factors had differing motivational weights for different individuals. For instance, Mr. Nowell unquestionably found his major satisfaction in the meticulous performance of his traditional obligations, whereas Mr. Whonnuck patently enjoyed the gamesmanship aspects of his potlatch relationships.

Functions and origins

Speculation as to origins of social institutions does not invariably contribute to the understanding of the institutions concerned. In the present case, however, it seems worthwhile to give brief consideration to the matter of origins for two reasons. First, the potlatch has a superficial appearance of being a cultural anomaly, or at least it has been so presented by some writers; and second, our present data and certain other materials on record suggest that it should be possible to factor out certain concepts in Southern Kwakiutl, and then general

Northwest Coast culture, that seem to have provided the basis on which the potlatch complex developed. The essential purpose here is to stress the interpretation of the potlatch as a fairly rational development rather than as a cultural monstrosity, understandable only in terms of psychologic aberrations among its partisans.

Fairly recently Suttles (1960a, b) has contributed two papers on certain features of culture of Coast Salish divisions of lower Vancouver Island and opposite mainland shores, groups included in the linguistic groupings Lkongeneng and Halkomelem.[41] From his data he has drawn conclusions as to the function and origin of the potlatch among these groups and, by extension, to the origin of the potlatch in Northwest Coast areal culture. His study represents the first new approach to the subject since Barnett's analysis. While we do not accept certain of Suttles' conclusions, we agree with a part of his interpretation as indicating a functional factor in the probable origin of the potlatch. We shall therefore use his work as a springboard to clarify our views.

Suttles' approach to the Coast Salish potlatch and its underlying factors is in terms of economic determinism; this is a part of his interpretation with which we are not in accord. He regards the potlatch itself as a device for redistributing wealth goods that tended to concentrate in the hands of certain especially favored or fortunate local groups. He stresses the fact that Coast Salish subsistence economy was derived from a region characterized by great variability in natural resources, a variability manifested both geographically—basic foodstuffs having spotty distributions in the several localities and biotic zones—and temporally, according to season and in regard to salmon from year to year in accordance with greatly varying spawning cycles. Thus, at any given time, as Suttles depicts the situation, some Coast Salish groups would be enjoying abundance while others were on short rations. These inequities were countered by a special social custom, according to which surplus food products were taken to affinal kindred as gifts. Such food

[41] For convenience Suttles refers to these groups simply as "Coast Salish."

gifts, however, obligated the recipients to make a return gift of "wealth goods." Suttles distinguishes wealth in food from that in more durable materials. It was not actually a barter system, but it operated like one. Suttles presents it as a commercial sort of transaction through which groups temporarily possessing food surpluses acquired credits in the form of durable wealth goods with which they, in their time of scarcity, would discharge their obligations when they were similarly presented with food gifts. At this point Suttles emphasizes the importance of the network of affinal relationships that interconnected all the local groups of the linguistic entities of his study. These affinal relationships provided the basis for all social contact beyond that of the local group of blood kin.

As the next step, he envisages certain groups, through greater industry, luck, or skill, as having more frequent surpluses of food than their affinal kin, so that they had a favorable balance of trade leading to acquiring wealth goods over and above their needs for repaying food gifts. Hence the wealth goods tended to accumulate in their hands. The potlatch served to remedy the stagnation of the wealth system that would otherwise have resulted by providing a mechanism for redistributing this wealth, so that the essential process, the exchange of food for wealth goods which leveled off the inequalities of the natural resources, might continue indefinitely.

In extending his consideration beyond Coast Salish territory, Suttles proposes the same function for the potlatch, subject to differences in group composition resulting from the seriation of social rank among the Wakashan-speaking peoples, so that the potlatch also becomes "the means by which individuals and local groups establish and maintain rank within the series," and to differences imposed by the most rigid group definition of all, that of the unilateral descent groups of the northern portion of the coast.

Discussion of Suttles' hypothesis must necessarily begin with consideration for the food-for-wealth exchange system between affinal kin. As a sort of side issue, Suttles posits a comparable diversity of local resources north of Salish territory to that of the Coast Salish, which would necessitate similar subsistence distribution mechanisms. He challenges generalizations as to the basic uniformity of Northwest Coast natural resources by way of substantiating his view.

Now, it is to be doubted that anyone who is reasonably familiar with the Northwest Coast and its native culture patterns would deny that there was considerable local diversity in natural resources. Such diversity ranged from gross environmental differences—as for example, the semi-inland habitats of groups such as the Chilkat Tlingit, the Gitksan, the Bella Coola, and various small units like the Nootkan a'minqasath as compared with the habitats of their neighbors of the outer coast and offshore islands—to local variations in resources resulting from specialized distributions of certain species of fish and game—the fact that olachon run in certain rivers only, as do sockeye salmon, and that there were no deer on the Queen Charlotte Islands and no red cedar in the Chilkat country. Pages could be filled with items of this sort. What the generalizations on uniformity of resources really mean is that throughout the area there was one important food source, salmon, which though seasonal lent itself to preservation for storage by use of a fairly simple technique. It may be stressed here that two species regarded by both Indians and ourselves as inferior in flavor, chums and pinks (colloquially, "dog salmon" and "humpbacks"), were of major importance to the natives, since both species ceased feeding for a considerable period prior to entering fresh water and hence were leaner and kept better than fat species such as spring salmon and coho. The same is probably true of sockeye taken in fresh water. While Suttles stresses the marked year-to-year difference in size of Frazer River sockeye runs, it may be doubted that primitive precommercial demands were so heavy that the smaller runs produced serious hardship. In any event, the year-to-year fluctuations in salmon were not characteristic of parts of the area other than those occupied by Coast Salish. The result of the natural features of the salmon fishery, in cultural terms, was an annual period of intensive economic activity by the natives, comparable in a broad sense to the busy harvest season of agricultural peoples.

Another important food source for all except riverine groups like the Gitksan was shellfish. Ethnographic accounts do not develop the importance of this humble, unspectacular resource, and Suttles incorrectly surmises that it may have been sparse and sporadic north of Salish territory. But one has only to observe the amazingly numerous and large midden deposits, composed chiefly of shell along the coast, to realize the utility of local mollusca in native economics (Drucker, 1943). There is a myth current in certain anthropological circles to the effect that there are no extensive midden sites in Tlingit territory. This, like other myths, is factually incorrect.

In addition, there were other aquatic resources. Some were seasonal, like herring and, in certain mainland rivers, olachon; and others were available throughout the year. There were also marine mammals—hair seal, sea lion, sea otter, porpoise, and whale. As a result, fishing and sea mammal hunting were major forms of economic activity. Concomitant with this economic pattern was a stress on water transport, and habitation patterns reflected this use of canoes, a favorable beach for landing being a most important consideration in the choice of a site throughout the area. Land hunting was less important in terms of subsistence, although mountain goat wool, marmot hides, and in historic times peltries were important valuables. This emphasis on river and sea as more important than the land in the food quest is an aspect of the broad uniformity of Northwest Coast native economy. The fact that the Nootkan staff of life was dog salmon, while the Haida wintered on dried humpbacks, does not materially alter the picture.

North of Salish territory,[42] the intergroup distribution of sporadically occurring food products was accomplished through barter. The most prominent center for barter was the Coast Tsimshian and Niska olachon fishing camps on the lower Nass, where Tlingit and Haida assembled to trade. But there was

[42] In contrasts between Coast Salish and non-Salish groups in the present discussion, it must be understood that we use "Coast Salish" precisely as Suttles does, that is, to refer to the Lkongeneng and Halkomelem dialectic entities; and furthermore, since in cultural terms the Bella Coola were highly similar to their Heiltsuk neighbors, we include them with the non-Salish, despite the fact of their actual linguistic affiliation, to avoid cumbersome special mention in each case of reference

other trade, apparently in short steps, between neighboring groups through which special foods like olachon grease as well as wealth goods were disseminated. The general impression one receives of this trade, however, is that both "wealth items" and foodstuffs involved in the exchanges were in the category of luxury goods and, contrary to Suttles' picture of the Coast Salish exchange system were not basic necessities for groups short of supplies. The Haida who came to the Nass to trade for olachon grease did not, it is true, have streams in their islands from which olachon could be taken. If, however, they actually needed all the animal fats they like to consume, they had local sources in the abundance of hair seal and sea lion, which they were highly skillful at hunting; the grease rich "black cod"; and other fish, including the spring salmon taken by trolling. In other words, the olachon grease they acquired at the Nass was over and above their actual dietetic needs. Some southern Tlingit, such as those having access to olachon fishing in the Unuk and Stikine rivers, went to the Nass for grease because the Nass olachon were reputed to have a superior flavor. We might justifiably compare them to people in our own culture who willingly pay a premium price for allegedly country-cured Virginia ham in preference to the standard Chicago packinghouse variety. There can be little doubt about the luxury aspect of such commerce.

The nearest approach to the formal Coast Salish food-for-wealth interchanges between affinally related groups among the non-Salish was the feast pattern. It is true that the Indians of the coast invariably distinguish between feasts and potlatches, both in terminology and in formal procedure, but it is likewise true that feasts and potlatches were intrinsically related conceptually. Both forms involved a host group and formally invited guest group or groups; both had elaborate etiquette patterns and were tied into the system of protocol of rank. The Wakashan-speaking groups from whom we have detailed information, and probably all their neighbors as well, announced certain hereditary rights at feasts, comparable to those announced at potlatches. In the case of feasts, such rights included special feast names; and when the food had come from hereditarily owned tracts (fishing places, berry grounds, hunting areas, and so forth), that fact and the genealogical route of transmission to the current possessors were announced. Where the food did not come from owned areas but had been taken through inherited knowledge, both practical and magical—as, for instance, in the case of Nootkan whaling—the source and line of descent of such knowledge was recounted, just as at a potlatch the origin and inheritance of a mask, a dance performance, and the like were formally presented before the guests. Finally, both feasts and potlatches involved consumption and distribution of surpluses assembled by the host chief with the aid of his group. We are referring here to the pattern described as the older one by Southern Kwakiutl informants prior to the development of individual giving of potlatches. At feasts, food was typically served not only for consumption on the spot, but in sufficient amount so that the guests would have plenty to take home. A chief might be given a very large amount so that he could distribute it to members of his group who had not been able to attend the formal affair. He was expected to explain to them the rights and so forth claimed by the giver and any other circumstances of the feast.

Feasts were normally given among groups that were in frequent, friendly contact: the several groups sharing a winter village or neighbors within a well-marked physiographic region, such as an inlet. These were essentially the groupings referred to by Southern Kwakiutl informants as those within which potlatches were given in former days. These were the groupings most frequently linked by intermarriage. There was no closely calculated system of reciprocity, but over the long haul feasts were returned, guest groups sooner or later inviting their former hosts. Among the matrilineal descent groups of the northern coast, guests had to be from a division with which the rule of exogamy permitted marriage.

There are two points that this summary of feast usages brings out. One is that there is no indication among Wakashan or northern groups of any rigorously formalized food-for-wealth system of food giving or feast giving. The other is that, similarly, there is no hint from any of these groups that the guests were hardship cases. Northwest Coast feasts were not CARE packages; the guests normally had food in plenty in their own storage boxes and baskets. One highly significant fact, insufficiently stressed in most of the literature, that does inevitably appear from informants' accounts is that feasts had considerable diversion value. They were usually occasions for jollity in contrast to potlatches, which were as a rule more formal and serious even when not directly part of mortuary observances.

If we return to Suttles' construct in terms of the general areal picture, then we must of necessity reach one or the other of two possible conclusions. The first possibility is that the Coast Salish had developed a highly specialized food distribution system, distinct from all other feast and food-giving customs of the area. The other possible conclusion is that Suttles' informants may have oversystematized their descriptions of this phase of native culture; they were members of groups that along with their congeners of Puget Sound and the Chinook have the longest history of intensive acculturation on the coast, dating back to the days of the crown colony of Vancouver Island, with a consequent awareness of white concepts of sale of commodities. This does not mean that such transactions were not made, particularly during the historic period, but that they may have been less commercialized. That is, groups with food surpluses may not have consistently singled out affinal kin who were suffering scarcity as recipients of the gifts in order to exact payments of wealth goods. As a matter of fact, Barnett, who had a couple of decades advantage in regard to Coast Salish informants, describes as customary a food-wealth exchange that went in part in the opposite direction from that reported by Suttles.[43] According to his account, in the Coast Salish equivalent of what we have referred to among the Kwakiutl as the "repayment of the bride price," the father of the bride took food gifts, or wealth goods that could be exchanged for food, as well as the wealth goods for the bride-price repayment. The food was given to the son-in-law or to his sponsor, so that the recipient might give a

[43] Reference is to Barnett (1955:180 ff., esp. 191–192). Suttles was apparently unfamiliar with this important source on the groups he studied since he does not refer to it.

feast in honor of the occasion to announce the rights and privileges being transferred by the father-in-law. The wealth goods that constituted the bride-price repayment had been transferred prior to the feast. When the father-in-law made ready to depart several days later, the son-in-law and his kin provided canoes loaded with food, which the father-in-law took to give a feast at his own home, announcing the food as a gift from his son-in-law. Derivatively he thereby acknowledged his own compliance with his obligation to repay the bride price.[44]

This description of a common expression of Coast Salish gift exchange between affinal relatives deserves a little closer examination, for Barnett makes clear that food gifts were made with the specific purpose that the recipient give a feast with the food received, at which he would inform the guests from whom and why he had received the food, thus publicizing and emphasizing the relationship between the two groups. This was not a Salish peculiarity. The use of food gifts we noted among the Southern Kwakiutl, and it was a fundamental Northwest Coast concept. Food gifts in quantity were to be redistributed by the recipient within his group at a feast and were never intended to be hoarded for rationing out in hard times. Thus, if we score the operation as described by Barnett, noting that it is more acceptable in terms of areal ideals and values than Suttles' interpretation, we find the following gains in calories: father-in-law, zero; son-in-law, zero. In terms of our thrift-biased economic reckoning, both actually lost, for the food each gave the other for feasts might have been stored away for use when supplies were short instead of being gormandized in the season of plenty. But what the persons in the exchange really gained was the strengthening of their formal affinal bond, and the informal but important public esteem that accrues to one in any culture who is punctilious in compliance with his social obligations.

Another problem that arises in connection with Suttles' interpretation of food-for-wealth exchanges between Coast Salish

[44] Barnett (1955:192–193) makes the point that the term "bride price" is not in accord with the Salish concepts of the transfers accompanying marriage. While accepting his qualification, we continue to use the term for convenience.

groups that served to counterbalance abundance and scarcity of natural resources relates to the prehistoric and even early historic intergroup relationships. It is obvious that to have the economic effect described by Suttles the exchanges had to be between distant groups, at least between groups inhabiting differing biotic zones, depending on different spawning cycles of salmon, etc. Variable as the Coast Salish habitat may have been, adjacent villages must have suffered the same scarcities and enjoyed the same abundances, so that food gifts to close neighbors could scarcely have had the effect posited. Yet Barnett (1955: 182, 267 ff.) makes clear that, while certain enclaves of adjacent groups usually maintained friendly relations among themselves, hostility was usual between more remotely situated units. He suggests that it was probably the enforcement of order by white authorities that led to the "abandonment of aboriginal group isolation" (p. 182). What we infer from this is that the situation among these groups was closely comparable to that among the Southern Kwakiutl, where small, exclusive groupings of neighboring social units gave feasts and potlatches only among themselves until relatively late historic times. That Suttles regards his "Coast Salish" as biologically a single population and culturally a single people, and that even aboriginally they may have established occasional affinal ties between distant units, are not significant factors. The Southern Kwakiutl were surely biologically and culturally a single people, and occasionally arranged marriages of state between scions of chiefly lines of remotely situated groups, but nonetheless they fought bitterly among themselves in ancient days. The same is known of the Nootkan tribes, of the Heiltsuk, where the groups that came to be known as the Bella Bella savagely persecuted their linguistic and cultural kindred, the Awikeno and the Xaihaid; and identical situations prevailed among the northern divisions of the coast. It is quite obvious that long-range, peaceful intercourse was nowhere part of the areal pattern. Thus, the network of affinal relationships linking all the Coast Salish that Suttles postulates could not very well have provided the channels for the sharing of the food wealth.

The next step proposed by Suttles, the concentration of

wealth goods in few hands as the result of the postulated exchanges, would not follow in any case unless it could be shown that there were certain garden spots in Coast Salish territory that always had surpluses; and in that case it would be expectable that only certain of the Coast Salish would indulge in giving potlatches. Their less fortunate affinal kindred would have had to dedicate all the wealth goods they could acquire to the repayment of the hypothetical food gift obligations. There is, however, no evidence at all to show that certain Salish groups only were hosts at potlatches, while the rest were chronically guests.

Significant error is introduced into Suttles' considerations regarding potlatch function by his reliance on the fallacious assumption that the giving of potlatches and feasts created high status.[45] In Barnett's general study of the potlatch, he made clear that this was not so; and in his descriptive account of Coast Salish cultures, including most of the same ethnic entities treated by Suttles, he demonstrates that among those people, as with others of the Northwest Coast, high social rank and control of wealth, food resources, and the personnel whose cooperation was essential to potlatching and feast-giving were simultaneous attributes of noble birth—that is, of inheritance of high status (Barnett, 1938; 1955:241–249, 250–266). Our present data from the Southern Kwakiutl make the same fact clear; even when, as informants asserted, in recent times lesser chiefs of the namima began to give potlatches, they did so on the basis of their recognized social rank. The only persons not originally hereditarily entitled to special status who were permitted to participate prominently in the potlatching were the eagles, and they had places artificially created for them. It is worth noting that even the eagle places were fitted into the mold of hereditary right; the places *became* hereditary privileges and were strictly regulated by the real chiefs who refused to permit more than a limited number of them to be established.

[45] Suttles (1960a:299) states, "high status comes from the sharing of food"; and (1960a:303) "wealth . . . is a means to high status achieved through the giving of it."

Suttles' observation that the potlatch was a means by which wealth was redistributed is valid, but we do not accept that it ever served, as he maintains, to accommodate local group economies to variation and fluctuation in natural resources. As we have indicated, aboriginal and early historical potlatching involved groups in geographical propinquity, so that there would rarely be significant variation in resources among them; and in addition, both potlatching and feasting, as well as other forms of food-giving, were matters of manipulating surpluses, not basic necessities. One way in which the Indians themselves express this latter point is in their insistence that in aboriginal times potlatches were of relatively infrequent occurrence whereas feasts were common. What they mean is that, prior to the introduction of the plethora of trade goods that came to be integrated into their wealth system (blankets, and so forth), accumulation of a surplus adequate for even a modest potlatch was a slow and painstaking process. The same principle operated in modern times among the Southern Kwakiutl. As the earning power of these people expanded with the growth of the canned salmon industry, their potlatching burgeoned, despite severe administrative pressures against it. There was, however, a lull during the Depression years; only a few chiefs who had been saving potlatch capital for years previous could give feasts and potlatches during this period. Another lull followed the financially disastrous fishermen's strike in 1936, when most Southern Kwakiutl, at the end of what should have been their major earning season, found themselves not only with scant funds but heavily in debt. We may surmise that correspondingly in ancient times an occasional failure of a salmon run or other basic resource would have inhibited the giving of feasts; and if there had been access to provisions by barter, this use would have cut into the accumulation of surpluses of wealth goods also.

While we disagree sharply with Suttles' interpretation of the potlatch as a device for leveling off inequities in natural resources among the tribes, it is only proper to recognize that he presents in reasonable terms his data on the diversity, permanent and occasional, of food resources in the Coast Salish habitat. Such is not the case in Piddocke's (1965) attempt to apply the same hypothesis to Southern Kwakiutl potlatching.

Piddocke (an early draft of whose proposition was followed by Vayda [1961]) carries Suttles' appraisal of economic diversity as a factor contributory to the potlatch to extremes by asserting that the Southern Kwakiutl lived constantly on the verge of starvation, warded off only by the food-for-wealth exchanges from which he derives the institutionalized potlatch. That these or any other Northwest Coast people lived with the specter of starvation perpetually leering over their shoulders is absurd.

To begin, Suttles' thesis of diversity of resources in Coast Salish country derives in part at least from the circumstances that the Coast Salish occupied in the main two specialized biotic regions that differed climatologically and in flora and fauna from the rest of the British Columbia coast. We do not accept these differences as forming the basis for the origin of the potlatch, as does Suttles, but they certainly were reflected in Coast Salish economy. The "Coast Forest Biotic Area" (all Vancouver Island west of Sooke and north of Comox and the mainland north of Burrard Inlet) differed in various ways. Suttles (1960b) has elucidated these differences. While there were rather less edible vegetal products available to the natives, there is no evidence of the drastic cyclic fluctuations in the fisheries recorded for the "Gulf Islands Biotic Area." Fluctuations in fish populations do occur, but they are random, less frequent, and proportionately smaller than in the pink and sockeye salmon runs in Salish territory. This suggests that variability of water temperatures on the spawning grounds and the other environmental conditions that ichthyologists cite are more stable in the Coast Forest zone, so that reproduction-and-survival rates quickly reestablish affected populations. The obvious corollary is that the enormous demand of modern commercial fishing is of more significance in creating annual variation with occasional seasons of poor fishing in Kwakiutl territory and to the northward rather than in the Coast Salish region; hence in pre-commercial times years of scarcity must have been even less common than in modern days.

Thus, in short, Piddocke's construct of the famine-ridden

Kwakiutl does not make sense. The classical anthropological picture of the Northwest Coast as a region prodigal in foodstuffs for its primitive inhabitants must stand as essentially correct. The idea of the potlatch as a sort of intertribal AID program to combat starvation does not fit the ecological facts.

This is not to deny that there were now and again times of food shortage in the midst of this plethora of abundance. But these were short periods of skimpy rations and discomfort but not of abject starvation. Men's bellies rumbled, small children cried, but no one actually starved to death. Drucker (1951:36–37) has reported such situations among the Nootkans, caused often by mismanagement of provisions—spectacular waste in feasting on winter stores—followed by stormy weather that made ground fishing (for cod, halibut, etc.) and sea hunting impossible. Land game in such periods lies low in such shelter as it can find and is difficult to encounter. The Nootkans whose habitat was more exposed to the lash of the tremendous seas of southeasterly storms—the principal source of heavy weather on the Northwest Coast—suffered more from such weather than did most of their neighbors, except for the Kwakiutl Quatsino Sound groups and those of storm-beaten Cape Scott. But there was always something to be found even in such periods. "Those were the times when people walked the beaches looking for codfish heads, spurned by seals and sea lions, and storm-killed herring, and pilchard. They collected and ate the tiny mussels of the inner coves and bays, and similar molluscs disdained in normal times" (Drucker, 1951). A tough, rank-flavored seagull may be nothing to make a gourmet's eyes glisten, but it will sustain life in a pinch. These birds congregate in sheltered coves in bad weather. The Indians shot them with arrow, clubbed them, or caught them on small fishhooks baited with shallow water molluscs.

The point of this argument is to develop a series of facts that combine to invalidate Piddocke's theory of the potlatch as a defense against starvation:

1. Periods of food shortage among the Indians of the Coast Forest Biotic Area were infrequent and limited principally to periods of heavy storms, when winter stores were exhausted so

that the people depended on day-to-day food procurement.

2. Even at such times there were food sources, not tasty perhaps, but sufficient to stave off abject starvation.

3. When one group was subject to such hardship conditions, stormbound in other words, all their neighbors were too—southeasters are general storms on the coast, not local—so that groups having surplus provisions could not have come to the rescue of neighbors in short supply.

In addition there is no evidence whatsoever of ceremonious food-for-wealth exchanges among the Southern Kwakiutl. For certain products of limited natural occurrence like olachon (specifically, the grease derived from them) or of special local abundance like the Cape Scott halibut, the concept of buying and selling ("bartering" would be more precise) existed, that is, of transfers in a mercantile, not ceremonial, context. Piddocke himself, cites various passages from Boas' writings to this effect. This "interconvertibility of food, wealth, and prestige" does not provide a *source* for the institutionalized potlatch, hence Piddocke is eventually forced to assume the existence of the potlatch (1965:259 ff.).

Finally, the point made in connection with Suttles' interpretation of the Coast Salish situation regarding feast and ceremonious food-gift patterns (as distinct from mercantile barter) applies to Piddocke's food distribution for survival: food given at feasts and in ceremonious distribution was not given to be hoarded by recipients against hard times but to be expended promptly by them—gormandized—in feasting. The obvious import of this is that food gifts were surpluses, not necessary to survival, to both the donors and the recipients. Piddocke's construct, in fine, in no way conforms to the facts of Southern Kwakiutl life.

Thus far we seem to have been highly critical of Suttles' views. His emphasis on the importance of the affinal relationship, however, provides a significant lead as to conceptual sources contributing to the base on which the potlatch complex seems to have developed. This very special social relationship had not been given adequate attention previously. It is a kinship behavior form that is more subtle than a joking relation-

CONCLUSION 151

ship or mother-in-law avoidance, but it was quite as real and, moreover, had far-reaching significance in the total configuration of Northwest Coast society.

Suttles sought to contrast the effects of the affinal relationship among the Coast Salish with what he calls "seriation" among Wakashan-speaking groups, because data on this point from these latter peoples were not available, although Drucker (1951) gave the matter mention in dealing with Nootkan society. However, present data from the Southern Kwakiutl show that this aspect of kinship behavior was significantly operative among them also, as among their neighbors. The informant Whonnuck's appeal to the recalcitrant tawitsis, that they alter their plans so as to permit completion of his father's potlatch, revolved about this relationship. It was the intimate bond between father-in-law and son-in-law that made the elder Whonnuck's trick, through which he made a son-in-law bend double and thus symbolically break a copper for the man's own father-in-law, especially malicious and insulting to both men. The giving of a potlatch to the entire tribe from which the wife came, as a form of payment of the bride price—thus making her entire tribe, rather than just her namima, affinal kin—was another Kwakiutl way of expressing the store that they set on this relationship. The ancient potlatching groups were simultaneously the normally intermarrying groups, although even in ancient times some unions were arranged between distant groups by chiefs bold enough and with a large enough supporting force of warriors to dare to approach remote, unfriendly villages openly. It was just these old, long-range affinal ties that were seized upon to justify expansion of the potlatch groupings when white-enforced peace began to make distant visits safe. In brief, our data show plainly that the affinal relationships were just as socially significant among the Southern Kwakiutl as among Coast Salish.

Suttles is on firm ground once more when he points out the important functional relationship between the unilateral descent system of the northern peoples where the affinal groupings were in effect crystallized by the clan and moiety organizations and the potlatch reciprocity. That he suggests derivation of the unilateral descent system from potlatch reciprocity is something else again—the argument deteriorates into something comparable to that as to the priority of the chicken or the egg—but there is no question at all but that the two institutions have a high degree of functional compatibility. In fine, throughout most of the area of distribution of the potlatch complex—all of that region from which we have reasonably complete data—we find marked accent on importance of affinal relationships and potlatch reciprocity between groups standing in such relation to each other.

In an attempt to point to function factors contributing to the development of the potlatch, the present writers would trace the pattern of formal relationships with affinal kin one step farther back; that is to say, to the establishment of such bonds by gift exchanges that formalized marriage. The marriage established the affinal bonds; the gift exchange set a behavior pattern for the newly linked social units.

Payment of some sort of bride price to legitimatize marriage, even though at times it was but a token, was a widespread enough practice in native North America so that its occurrence on an earlier phase of Northwest Coast culture might be assumed without much hazard. It is necessary only to point to certain qualifying precautions. One is, of course, that while terms such as "bride price" and "marriage by purchase" are often met with in the literature and are convenient, short designators, they are rarely if ever precise descriptions of the situation; for it seems clear that there was always a distinction between "purchase" of a wife and purchase of a chattel. It might be possible to argue on purely hypothetical grounds that the "repayment" of the bride price as practiced by the Wakashan-speaking groups and most Coast Salish represented a defense against what we might call a strictly commercialized transaction. Be that as it may, the gift exchanges manifestly defined a pattern for the future relationships of the two groups involved.

A second precaution is that, for an interpretation of the significance of such gift exchanges as providing part of the structural base of the potlatch, it becomes necessary to assume in addition the prior existence of a wealth system consisting of food surpluses and of utilitarian and/or nonutilitarian objects regarded as worth possessing. Such an assumption does not seem to offer major difficulty in view of the various forms of wealth systems that we know to have been developed in various parts of the world, even though no two of them may have been quite alike in meaning and function.

The final major factor, the one which we believe must have been present in order that the preceding concepts be structured into the rudiments of the potlatch, is a little more complex. The gift exchanges could have been little more than a casual and inconsequential kinship usage unless this practice was linked to a concept of inheritance of rights and an equation of possession of such rights with social status. The invariable purpose of the potlatch, that of presenting claims to hereditary rights, manifestly means that such a concept was basic. We can go a bit further and suggest that the early form of the potlatch may well have been that at which the deceased chief was replaced by his successor, providing the basis through which, in the northern section of the coast, the mortuary and memorial aspects of the affair seem at times to outweigh the presentation of the heir—although invariably the heir formally claimed his inheritance at the occasion. As guests, the affinal kindred saw the heir, in whom they had a direct interest, presented as the claimant to the rights that they knew were his due. The potlatch gifts distributed to them may be considered a repetition of the "bride price," representing a desire to continue the friendly bond between the two groups. Or, a little more imaginatively, those gifts may have been the final payment of the transaction; perhaps the heir was what his father's group was really "buying" when they first began to arrange the marriage. That this idea is not as far-fetched as it might seem at first glance is suggested by the Nootkan emphasis on an heir or heirs as essential to the completion of the marriage arrangements. If a married couple separated or had no issue, the various wealth goods payments were not returned, that is, there was no cash refund; but, and this is the significant point, all rights and privileges formally bestowed by the bride's father at the time of the bride-price repayment reverted to him (and his group).

What we have been trying to say in these final pages is this: We do not accept economic determinism as the origin of the potlatch; we do not believe that it was devised to assist distant hostile groups in solving their subsistence problems, nor to keep wealth goods circulating. Neither do we believe that it could have sprung into being full-blown as a technique for conspicuous consumption by paranoiacs. Rather we believe that the complex probably developed gradually through a fusion of certain simpler concepts mutually compatible in function. As possible basic components, we have pointed to gift exchange at marriage, leading into a continuing special relationship between affinal kin, a wealth system, the concept of inheritance of rights associated with social status, and the formal presentation of the heir at the mortuary rites in honor of a deceased chief. These concepts themselves may have been expanded as the new complex grew, and thus explain the rights elaborated by fancies lifted from mythologies, or the statuses increased in number and seriated in rank. We believe that this hypothesis offers a modicum of intelligibility into possible origins of the potlatch, which was, after all, a rather peculiar social institution.

Bibliography

ALLEN, R. M.
  1956 The Potlatch and Social Equilibrium. Davidson Journal of Anthropology, Vol. 2, No. 1, pp. 43–54. Seattle.
BARNETT, HOMER G.
  1938 The Nature of the Potlatch. American Anthropologist, n.s., 40:349–358.
  1955 The Coast Salish of British Columbia. University of Oregon Monographs, Studies in Anthropology, No. 4. University of Oregon Press, Eugene.
  n.d.   The Nature of the Potlatch. Doctoral dissertation (unpubl.), University of California, Berkeley.
BENEDICT, RUTH F.
  1932 Configurations of Culture in North America. American Anthropologist, n.s., 34:1–27.
  1934 Patterns of Culture. Houghton Mifflin, Boston and New York.
BLAU, PETER
  1964 Exchange and Power in Social Life. John Wiley, New York, London, and Sydney.
BOAS, FRANZ
  1897 The Social Organization and the Secret Societies of the Kwakiutl Indians. Report of the U.S. National Museum for 1895, Washington.
BOHANNAN, PAUL
  1963 Social Anthropology. Holt, Rinehart and Winston, New York.
CODERE, HELEN
  1950 Fighting with Property. American Ethnological Society, Monograph No. 18.
  1956 The Amiable Side of Kwakiutl Life. American Anthropologist, n.s., 58:334–351.
  1957 Kwakiutl Society: Rank Without Class. American Anthropologist, n.s., 59:473–486.
  1959 The Understanding of the Kwakiutl. In W. Goldschmidt (ed.), The Anthropology of Franz Boas. American Anthropological Association, Mem. No. 89:61–75.
  1961 Kwakiutl. In E. H. Spicer (ed.), Perspectives in American

Indian Culture Change, pp. 431–516. University of Chicago Press, Chicago.

CURTIS, EDWARD S.
1915 The Kwakiutl. The North American Indian, Vol. 10, Norwood, Conn.

DAWSON, G. M.
1887 Notes and Observations on the Kwakiuool People... Royal Society of Canada, Trans., Vol. 5, sec. ii.

DRUCKER, PHILIP
1940 Kwakiutl Dancing Societies. University of California Anthrop. Records, 2:201–230.
1943 Archaeological Survey on the Northwest Coast. Bureau of American Ethnology, Bull. 133, Washington.
1951 The Northern and Central Nootkan Tribes. Bureau of American Ethnology, Bull. 144. Washington.
1955 Indians of the Northwest Coast. American Museum of Natural History, Anthropological Handbook, No. 10.
1965 Cultures of the North Pacific Coast. Chandler Publishing Co., San Francisco.

FORD, CLELLAN S.
1941 Smoke from Their Fires. Yale University Press, New Haven.

HALLIDAY, W. M.
1935 Potlatch and Totem. J. M. Dent, London and Toronto.

HERSKOVITS, MELVILLE
1952 Economic Anthropology. Alfred A. Knopf, New York.

KEITHAHN, E. L.
1964 Origin of the "Chief's Copper" or "Tinneh." Anthropological Papers of the University of Alaska, 12:59–78.

LA VIOLETTE, FORREST E.
1961 The Struggle for Survival. Toronto University Press, Toronto.

PIDDOCKE, S.
1965 The Potlatch System of the Southern Kwakiutl. Southwestern Journal of Anthropology, 21:244–264.

SMITH, MARIAN W.
1959 Boas' "Natural History" Approach to Field Method. *In* W. Goldschmidt (ed.), The Anthropology of Franz Boas. American Anthropological Association, Mem. No. 89:46–60.

SUTTLES, WAYNE
1960a Affinal Ties, Subsistence, and Prestige Among the Coast Salish. American Anthropologist, 62:296–305.

1960b Variation in Habitat and Culture on the Northwest Coast. Trans. of the 34th International Congress of Americanists, pp. 522–537, Vienna.

VAYDA, A.
1961 A Re-examination of Northwest Coast Economic Systems. Trans. of the New York Academy of Sciences, 23:618–624.

VOGET, FRED W.
1956 The American Indian in Transition. American Anthropologist, n.s., 58:249–263.

WIKE, JOYCE
1952 The Role of the Dead in Northwest Coast Culture. *In* Sol Tax (ed.), Indian Tribes of Aboriginal America, Selected Papers of the 29th Congress of Americanists, pp. 97–103, University of Chicago Press, Chicago.
1957 More Puzzles on the Northwest Coast. American Anthropologist, n.s., 39:301–317.

Index

Alcohol, 85
Allen, R., 17

Barnett, H., 1, 4, 8, 70, 111, 116, 134, 143, 145, 146
Benedict, R., 3, 112
Blau, P., 136
Boas, F., 1, 10, 13, 40, 124
Bohannan, P., 1
Bride price, 39, 58, 70 ff., 144, 152

Cannibal Dance (Hamatsa), 32, 81, 87
Chieftainship, 11
Codere, H., 2, 4, 10, 13, 17, 19, 23, 24, 35, 37, 45, 64, 125
Colson, E., 1
Confederacies, 12, 16, 100
Crests, 26
Curtis, E., 3, 32

Double return, 53 ff.

Festival group, 40 ff.
Foods as wealth items, 138 ff., 144, 148
Ford, C., 6, 83

Genealogies, 10

Halliday, W., 30, 48, 50
Hammel, E., 1
Herskovits, M., 1
Hunt, G., 2, 25

Indian Act prohibiting potlatching, 27, 29, 87
Inheritance, validated through potlatch, 8, 132, 134, 154

Keithahn, E., 15
Kroeber, A., 6

La Violette, F., 29, 30
Loans, interest on and repayment of, 55, 58 ff., 69

Maquinna, Nootka chief, 31

Nativistic cults, 21

Pentacostal Church, 23
Piddocke, S., 5, 72, 148
Potlatch, meaning of term, 8
Potlatch, types of: grease feasts, 34, 65, 76; mortuary potlatch, 77, 130 ff.; rivalry potlatch, 98 ff., 118 ff.
Potlatch gifts: canoes, 62, 67; cash and checks, 63 ff.; coppers, 14, 44, 50, 58 ff., 68, 76, 78, 105, 119 ff., 127, 131; flour, 34, 38, 121; food, 144; furs, 92; trade blankets, 14, 57, 72, 79
Potlatch positions, 24, 46, 88, 99

Roberts, F., 1

Salish, 42, 137
Salmon, as food resource, 139 ff.
Smith, M., 2
Suttles, W., 5, 137 ff., 151

Vayda, A., 5, 148
Voget, F., 21

Warfare as substitute for potlatch, 18 ff., 125 ff.
Wike, J., 2, 54, 130

Printed in the USA
CPSIA information can be obtained
at www.ICGtesting.com
LVHW041150101023
PP17922000018B/119